The Historic
Country Hotels of England

A Select Guide

WENDY ARNOLD

The Historic
Country Hotels of England

A Select Guide

Photographs by
ROBIN MORRISON

Revised edition

CHRONICLE BOOKS

SAN FRANCISCO

For Mick

Frontispiece: A liveried hall-porter waits to take up your luggage at the gracious wrought-iron gates of Middlethorpe Hall, near York. See p.21.

Opposite: Dinner is laid at the Lake District hotel Miller Howe. The walls of the dining room were painted by the Italian artist Stefano Ficalbi in 1979. See p.17.

Revised edition published in the United States 1989 by Chronicle Books.

Printed and bound in Italy by Amilcare Pizzi, Milan.

Library of Congress Cataloging-in-Publication Data
Arnold, Wendy.
    The historic country hotels of England : a select guide/Wendy Arnold; with 120 color photographs by Robin Morrison.—Rev. ed.
        p. cm.
        Includes index.
        ISBN 0-87701-627-5
        1. Hotels, taverns, etc.—England—Guide-books.   I. Title.
    TX907.5.G72E542   1989
    647'.944101—dc 19

88-37341
CIP

Distributed in Canada by
Raincoast Books,
112 East Third Avenue,
Vancouver, B.C. V5T 1C8

10 9 8 7 6 5 4 3 2 1

Chronicle Books
275 Fifth Street
San Francisco, CA 94103

Contents

Preface

A romantic view of Le Talbooth, a luxury retreat in the very heart of Constable country. See p. 35.

English country house hotels come in all shapes and sizes: a luxuriously furnished battlemented castle, where Henry VIII entertained Anne Boleyn; an elegant Edwardian country mansion, where Noël Coward wrote *Hay Fever*; one of Sir Edwin Lutyens's finest masterpieces, complete with a garden by Gertrude Jekyll; a manor house of golden Cotswold stone, next door to the village church.

They can be vast, elegant, formal mansions standing in many acres of parkland, or tiny thatched cottages staffed by local village girls. Some claim to have ghosts; some are castles; some will organize pheasant shooting or trout fishing; and some are run by families whose ancestors have lived in them for four centuries or more. Above all, most are people's homes.

Here are staff who remember names, food that has never been frozen, and comfortable rooms in lovely, individual houses where visitors can feel they are staying with particularly thoughtful, caring friends.

As an English woman living abroad, I was frequently asked by friends for information about the best and most historic country hotels in England. I was astonished to find, when home for a visit, that some much-vaunted hotels were dreadful, and that some little-known ones were excellent. Intrigued, I set out on months of research and discovery, driving thousands of miles, never telling owners what I was doing until I paid my bill, and accepting no special treatment. The result was the first edition of this book.

For this revised edition of *The Historic Country Hotels of England*, I went back and inspected the hotels I had chosen, checked out new establishments as they opened, and continued my search for others that I might have missed. My standards are based on thirty years of setting up house in places as far apart as Khartoum and Santiago, running large households, and entertaining for my oil-executive husband, as well as four years of living in the USA and many years of visiting the world's finest hotels.

I have selected hotels that are historically and architecturally interesting, in lovely countryside, with marvellous chefs and delightful decor. The owners must be warmly welcoming, and the hotel has to be efficiently run, so that everything is spotlessly clean, service is rapid, bedrooms are comfortable and tastefully furnished, and bathrooms excellent, with plenty of hot water. Most importantly, they have to be places where everybody cared. There seems to be little point in staying anywhere, no matter how quaint, where I would pay to be less comfortable than at home. Maintaining high standards in what is often a very old building, training local staff, and coping with the English weather make great demands on the owners. All but three of the hotels I have selected for this book are run by their owners, and those three have dedicated managers willing to be involved twenty-four hours a day.

On my travels I rediscovered the pleasures of the English countryside: innumerable ancient villages and their churches, gardens great and small, stately homes. I continue to be delighted by the excellence of young British chefs, and am pleased to be able to report that many of the hotels I had chosen for the first edition are even better than before and have again been included.

The hotels in this book, like the English landscape, vary from the magnificent to the modest. They cover the whole of England and offer a peaceful place to stay even near the big cities; any of them can be reached within a day from London. Here is a personal selection of the hotels I have most enjoyed, and to which I would with confidence send even my most demanding friends.

Preparation Reservations are essential for all the hotels described and should be made as many months in advance as possible. Opening times should be checked: some hotels close for a day or more every week and many are not open in winter. Since ideas of comfort vary, be very specific about your requirements. If you want a six-foot double bed, a scenic view, or room and closet space for numerous bags, or if you find stairs a problem, follow a special diet, or are travelling with friends and want similar accommodation to theirs, say so when making reservations. Many hotels have good wall-mounted showers, but some have tubs only. These hotels were once private houses, so nothing is standard, which is their great charm. Rooms vary in size and view but should be priced accordingly. Good months to travel are May and October, which can have splendid weather. Children are back at school, roads are less crowded, and there is the added bonus of spring blossom and autumnal colors. No season in England is predictable, however, so it is always worth taking layers of clothing to build up or down, and a light raincoat. Jacket and tie are normally worn for dinner in all these hotels.

Terms Since prices can fluctuate, I have given only general guidelines. The hotels are divided into four categories, based on the price for two people sharing a room for one night and having dinner (without wine) and continental breakfast. I have included the government Value Added Tax of 15% and added 10% service, which some quote separately. Enquire when booking whether prices include both of these. (The dollar equivalent is based on a rate of exchange of £1.00 = $1.80.)

Moderate	£80–110 (approx. $144–198)
Medium	£115–155 (approx. $207–279)
Expensive	£160–195 (approx. $288–351)
Very Expensive	£200–240 (approx. $360–432)

This does not include à la carte meals, drinks, phone calls, or, except where stated, a full English breakfast. Some hotels offer reductions for stays of two days or longer, and many have special off-season rates. All-inclusive holiday or sporting programs may also be available. Enquire when booking.

Getting there I have included directions and approximate journey times for those travelling by car from London. Some hotels are accessible by rail, or are near airports. I have indicated helicopter landing facilities, where available (notice must always be given). Rental cars should be booked ahead of time.

Some hotels will arrange this, or provide a chauffeur-driven car for touring.

Sightseeing Most of these hotels provide good advice and information about their area. I have added a few notes about nearby places of interest. For more details, *Historic Houses, Castles and Gardens in Great Britain and Ireland*, published annually and available at larger bookstores and news-stands, gives county-by-county information, with admission fees and opening days and times. Many of the finest historic sites belong to a private body, the National Trust. Membership, available at each Trust property, gives free admission and helps support their upkeep. Keen gardeners will appreciate the National Gardens Scheme yellow booklet, *Gardens Open to the Public*, which also includes enchanting small private gardens open a few days each year for charity.

Eating out Not all hotels offer lunch, so I have suggested under "Refreshments" picturesque pubs or small restaurants for a quick meal, or in some cases dinner. In "Dining out" I have mentioned more formal places. Restaurants' reputations tend to alter rapidly, so check their current status with your hotel. NB More remote hotels include dinner in their prices.

Private houses I have included some private houses in this book, as I find them an attractive alternative to hotels. Anyone interested in staying in other similar homes should contact one of the organizations that centralize bookings and inspect recommended houses, such as: In the English Manner, Mawley House, Quenington, Nr Cirencester, Gloucestershire GL7 5BH, England, tel. Cirencester (0285) 75267 or Newport (0239) 77378, telex 940 12737 ITEM G.

Footnote What is so very pleasant about these hotels is that they provide a network of concerned people to help with any problems or queries that may arise as one travels round. An American lady wrote to tell me how one of the hotel managers not only tracked down the ancestral castle of her English forbears, but also arranged for a chauffeur-driven Mercedes to take her there with her daughter, and for them to lunch with their welcoming relatives. I am confident that the owners or managers of all the hotels I have chosen will be equally helpful and courteous at all times. It helps them to be told *personally* of any difficulties, and cheers them to hear of any specially pleasant surprises. I too should be very grateful to hear of them, care of the publishers.

An alphabetical index of hotels and their locations appears on page 96.

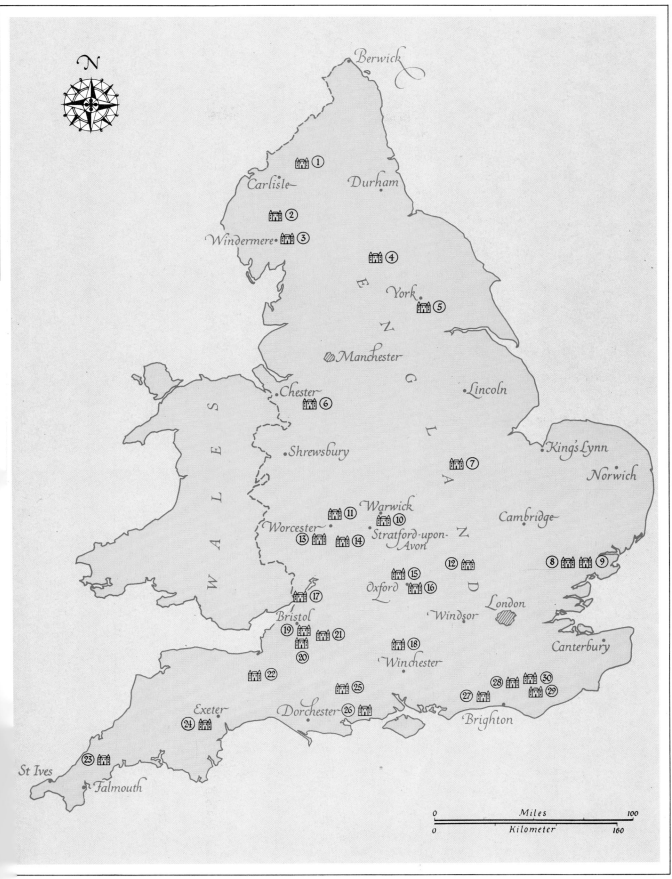

N

Berwick

Carlisle
Durham

② Windermere ③

④

York
⑤

Manchester

Chester
⑥

Lincoln

Shrewsbury

King's Lynn
Norwich

⑦

Warwick
⑪ ⑩
Worcester
Stratford-upon-Avon
⑬ Avon ⑭

Cambridge

⑧ ⑨

⑫
⑮
Oxford ⑯

London
Windsor

⑰
Bristol
Canterbury
⑲ ⑳ ㉑ ⑱
Winchester
㉒
㉕ ㉘ ㉚
㉗ ㉙
Exeter Dorchester ㉖ Brighton

㉔

㉓
St Ives
Falmouth

ENGLAND
WALES

0   Miles   100
0   Kilometer   160

A warm welcome in the Scottish borderland

The countryside in the far north of England is so wild and empty that it is an agreeable surprise to come across Farlam Hall. With its smooth green lawns, neat gravel drive, and well-tended gardens, it looks like an illustration from a Jane Austen novel. Wild ducks bob about placidly on the ornamental lake in front of it, unpinioned, beguiled by regular food and kind treatment. This site has been constantly occupied for over a thousand years; the oldest part of the present building was a farmhouse in the 1600s, as documents prove. John Wesley is said to have preached at Farlam Hall, and George Stephenson's famous locomotive, The Rocket, belonged to the owners, who used it to haul coal in the local mines until it was donated to London's Science Museum.

On chilly days, a fire burns cheerfully in the grate of Farlam Hall's small front room and the owners, the Quinion family, hasten to serve you welcome refreshments beside it once you have settled in. The bedrooms are comfortable, warm, cheerful, and well-stocked with small thoughtful extras. The modest proportions of the front part of the house deceive: dinner-time reveals a vast, high-ceilinged dining room and large drawing rooms, one of which has a huge *Alice Through the Looking Glass* mirror above the mantelpiece. Décor throughout is by Mrs Quinion. The food, briskly served in a friendly manner by family members, is fresh and tasty. The chef, the Quinions' son Barry, was trained in some notable establishments. Avocado mousse with red cabbage and Solway salmon finished with cucumber and mint sauce proved as delicious as they sounded, and the desserts on the sideboard tasted as good as they looked.

Many people who stay at Farlam Hall come to see the nearby well-preserved remains of Hadrian's

Wall, built right across England by the Romans AD 117–138 to keep out marauding tribes from Scotland. Others come to fish, shoot, walk, watch birds, explore the Lake District or Scottish Borders, or merely to break their journey on the way north or south. Mr Quinion told me, diffidently, that guests who come for a night often stay for a week, and then return year after year. Farlam Hall is an unpretentious, comfortable, and warmly welcoming family concern.

Opposite: wild ducks on the lake outside the hotel, a sun-lit lounge, and a corner of the garden. Above: dinner is laid overlooking the lawns.

FARLAM HALL, Hallbankgate, Brampton, Nr Carlisle, Cumbria CA8 2NG. **Tel.** Hallbankgate (069 76) 234/359. **Telex** No. **Owners** The Quinion and Stevenson families. **Open** All year, except Feb. and Christmas. **Rooms** 12 double, 1 single, all with bathrooms (7 with tub and shower, 4 with tub only, 2 with shower only), direct-dial phone, color TV. NB 1 twin and 1 four-poster bedroom are on the ground floor. No elevator. **Facilities** 2 lounges, bar, dining room, 7-acre grounds, croquet. Golf nearby. **Restrictions** No children under 5. Dogs by prior arrangement with management only. **Terms** Moderate. All inclusive (dinner, room, full breakfast, VAT). Packed lunches, snacks, available to residents only by arrangement. Some special bargains late Oct.–April and reductions for stays of 2 days or longer. **Credit cards** Visa/Access/Amex. **Getting there** M1, M6 to Carlisle, A69 to Brampton. Hotel is on A689 2½ miles SE of Brampton, *not* in Farlam village. About 6 hrs. **Helicopter landing** No. **Of local interest** Hadrian's Wall; Lanercost Priory ruins; St Martin's Church, Brampton; Carlisle. **Whole day expeditions** Solway and Northumberland coasts; Lake District; Scottish Borders. **Refreshments** Hare 'n' Hounds, Talkin; The New Bridge, Lanercost. **Dining out** Sharrow Bay Hotel, Ullswater (see p.13).

Lakeside luxury

Sharrow Bay is not so much a hotel as a legend, the forerunner of, and model for, most of England's country house hotels. Few succeed in capturing anything like its own special charm. It is the country hotel preferred by the British above all others, and it is constantly winning awards which prove this, but the owners have never become complacent. They continue to care about every crumb that leaves their kitchen, and every guest that enters their door.

In 1949 Francis Coulson bought the little gray-stone 1840s house, which has a stupendous view down Ullswater. He was joined by Brian Sack three years later. From humble beginnings as a small hotel famous for its home-made fare, Sharrow Bay has acquired a devoted staff and a varied and deliciously self-indulgent menu. Cottages and a lakeside farm now provide extra rooms. The garden has matured marvellously, and the cream bill has risen steadily into monthly thousands of pounds. Since neither owner can resist antique shops, every available corner has gradually been filled with their finds. Those who travel with much luggage should ask for a large room, because much of the storage space is already filled with board games, books, hair driers, and extra blankets – forty years of experience teaches you to know what your guests might have forgotten or might want. There is a teatray with delicate china and a cookie jar, a drinks fridge, and a bathroom stacked with little extras. Everywhere is immaculate, comfortable, and snug, with heavy velvet curtains and plump soft chairs.

Dinner is splendidly formal, with waiters in stiffly starched white jackets. The choices on the menu are agonizing, since you know that all the twenty-four or so starters are equally good. Happily the next two courses are without choice. I began with tomato and tarragon soup, followed by a morsel of halibut with a fish-shaped wisp of puff pastry, and then a damson sorbet in a tall glass. The main course, a plump little Yorkshire grouse, came ringed with apple, celery, onions, bread sauce, fried breadcrumbs, allumette potatoes, redcurrant jelly, and game gravy – and that was *before* the vegetables arrived! A further impossible decision had to be made between fourteen mouth-watering desserts. I finally decided on a Regency syllabub. Coffee, cheese, and sweetmeats followed. All delectable and all prepared with an *Upstairs, Downstairs* lavish use of butter, cream, and eggs. The especially well-chosen wine-list matches the high quality of the food.

It is worth getting up early to enjoy the view down Ullswater and the smell of freshly baked croissants and brioches. The traditional British breakfast is of course superb. This is the sort of hotel that English children at boarding school, eating almost inedible food and sleeping on narrow lumpy beds, fantasize about, and that visitors from abroad, used to quantity-controlled portions, marvel at.

Opposite: a blazing fire makes the comfortable interiors even cozier. Above: one of the charming bedrooms. Overleaf: the hills surrounding Ullswater are a spectacular setting for the hotel.

SHARROW BAY COUNTRY HOUSE HOTEL, Lake Ullswater, Penrith, Cumbria CA10 2LZ. **Tel.** Pooley Bridge (085 36) 301. **Telex** No. **Owners** Francis Coulson and Brian Sack. **Open** Early March–early Dec. **Rooms** 24 double, 4 single, 7 cottage suites. All but 4 with bathroom with tub (none with shower). All with phone, radio, color TV, 14 with minibar, some with tea-making facilities. **Facilities** 5 lounges, breakfast room, restaurant, 12-acre grounds and woodlands, $\frac{1}{2}$-mile lake shore with private jetty and boathouse. **Restrictions** No dogs. No children under 12. No smoking in dining rooms. **Credit cards** No. Personal checks only. **Terms** Very expensive. Breakfast, VAT and service included. Lunch available. **Getting there** M1 (or M4, M5), then M6, Exit 40, A592 to Pooley Bridge. Hotel about 2 miles to the s. About $5\frac{1}{2}$ hrs. **Helicopter landing** Yes (24 hrs notice). **Of local interest** Wordsworth's homes; walking, climbing, lake bathing, fishing. **Whole day expeditions** Hadrian's Wall; Penrith; tours of Lakes, Pennines. **Refreshments** Pheasant, Bassenthwaite. **Dining out** Miller Howe, Windermere (see p.17).

A perfectly staged performance

John Tovey is the author of cookery books, a television personality, and a sometime theatrical entrepreneur, and his hotel, Miller Howe, has all the flair and flamboyant extravagance such a background might lead one to expect.

Perched high above Lake Windermere, in one of the most spectacular areas of the Lake District, the house is rather ordinary from the outside, but inside the reception rooms have the glamor and elegance of a Broadway stage setting. They glow with warm browns and creams, have heavy leather, brass-studded club armchairs and chesterfields, and at night look out over a floodlit garden, exotic with lush vegetation, fountains, and stone cupids. Inside are more cupids, some gilded, alcoves with dramatically lit displays of vivid blue Venetian and Bristol glass, and framed 18th-century silk embroidered panels. Vast arrangements of flowers are scattered throughout the hotel. The luxurious bedrooms are warmly centrally heated, close carpeted, and have trouser presses, hair driers, and glossy books about England thoughtfully provided. The glazed chintz matching bedcovers and curtains are tastefully patterned; bathrooms are sumptuous and have efficient showers and thick, huge towels warming on hot rails.

Dinner is An Event, for which guests are asked to assemble at 8.00, to choose wines over a cocktail, and be ready to move *en masse* to the dining room at 8.30 (there are two sittings on Saturdays). Once everyone is seated, the lights are lowered, and a file of young waiters whisks in the first of the many beautifully presented, interestingly flavored, and skilfully chosen courses. Daring ingredients and startling combinations are a feature of the menu, which begins always with a foreign speciality, followed by a soup, such as parsnip and ginger with pine nuts. The next course is fish – on my visit, the halibut cooked in yoghurt, accompanied by apple, fennel, celery, and peppers with cheddar cheese, was delicious. A garnished roast, ringed with at least seven vegetables, completes the "no choice" section of the meal, in which the tastes all perfectly balance and achieve a magnificent harmony. There is a mouth-watering selection of desserts, but beware of "My Nan's tipsy trifle," since there are the stairs to climb to bed.

After a comfortable night, you are greeted as you come downstairs in the morning with a generous goblet of Buck's Fizz, compliments of Mr Tovey. As you sit down to a perfectly prepared British breakfast, the whole panorama of mountains on the far side of the lake lies before you, and you may read their names on your menu. The highly talented Mr Tovey not only creates the original and delicious meals, but also designs the striking décor. A visit to Miller Howe is a theatrical experience, perfect in every detail, and must be unique in the hotel world.

Opposite: tea is served looking over Lake Windermere. Above: a drawing room gleams with leather furniture.

MILLER HOWE, Rayrigg Road, Windermere, Cumbria LA23 1EY. **Tel.** Windermere (096 62) 2536. **Telex No. Owner** John J. Tovey. **Manager** John Whalley. **Open** Early March–early Dec. **Rooms** 13 doubles, 10 with bathroom with tub and handshower, 1 with tub only, 2 with shower only, all with radio and cassette player. Color TV and portable phone available on request. **Facilities** 3 drawing rooms, 2 dining rooms, sun-lounge, terrace, 4-acre gardens. Laundry service (Mon.–Fri.). **Restrictions** No children under 12, no smoking in restaurant, no dogs in public rooms. **Terms** Expensive. Some autumn and spring special terms, occasional cookery courses with all-inclusive terms. **Credit cards** Visa/Diners/Amex/Access. **Getting there** M1 (or M4/M5) to M6, Exit 36 (signposted South lakes), A591 to Windermere until A592 turning on L, ¼ mile along road, watch carefully for hotel board. About 5 hrs. **Helicopter landing** No. **Of local interest** Carlisle; Holker Hall, Levens Hall, Sizergh Castle; gardens at Lingholm, Stagshaw, Acorn Bank. Craft shops, walking, trips on Lake steamers, climbing, sailing. **Whole day expeditions** Pennines; Lakes. **Refreshments** Pheasant, Bassenthwaite; Howe Town, Ullswater; Uplands, Cartmel; Miller Howe Kaff near Windermere train station. **Dining out** Sharrow Bay Hotel, Ullswater (see p.13).

Wake to birdsong in James Herriot's Yorkshire

Jervaulx Hall has a pleasing exterior. Its graceful façade has almost Dutch gables and long stately windows. There is an elegant clock-tower on the stables to the left, a pool with a pretty dolphin fountain in the center of its circular drive, and, to the right, lawns and flower borders, a croquet lawn and huge trees, and the path that leads into the romantic ruins of Jervaulx Abbey. The Hall is probably on the site of the Abbey guest-house; it has ancient cellars and some of the walls are over two feet thick. A glass porch contains a friendly jumble of tables and chairs and a box with croquet mallets. The comfortable and homely reception hall has a wood-burning stove and many helpful books and pamphlets for those who are touring. John Sharp, his daughter Elizabeth and their little dog, Scamp, will be waiting to welcome you.

The bedrooms are simple, with flowered wallpaper and a tea and coffee tray so that you can make yourself a hot drink. There will probably be a vase of wildflowers on the dressing table to greet you. Should you wish to telephone, there is a pay phone downstairs near the rather grand cloakroom. There is also a television in the hall, but nobody seems to bother to watch it. When you wake on a summer morning in fine weather, the birds are singing, and wild rabbits are playing on the lawn near the sundial. If you decide on a walk through the ruins, you will find wildflowers and trim paths, two huge weeping ash trees, walled courtyards and empty mullioned windows, wild roses rioting in pink and white profusion over the gray stones, and sheep grazing peacefully in the surrounding parkland.

Most guests spend the day touring the Yorkshire Dales. When I was there all the little towns were celebrating the five hundredth anniversary of the crowning of Richard III of York with as much enthusiasm as if it had happened in their lifetimes. Returning in the evening, guests will find John Sharp formally dressed in a suit waiting to take orders for

dinner. There is a modest wine-list and a choice between two dishes for each course. I enjoyed the onion and anchovy tart and the roast duckling; bowls of garden vegetables were brought round on a trolley and second helpings were encouraged. Profiteroles with chocolate sauce were followed by coffee in the drawing room, where we were joined by our host, and by Scamp, as we sat and exchanged Dales gossip. The conversation could have come straight from a James Herriot novel – indeed the author himself had dined there not long before. The other guests were, like our host, from the North, and when I asked them how long it might take me to drive back to London, everyone looked blank. Nobody had bothered to drive down there for years!

Opposite: a fountain plays outside Jervaulx Hall; the abbey ruins are close by. Above: a piano invitingly open in the drawing room.

JERVAULX HALL, Jervaulx, Masham, Nr Ripon, North Yorkshire HG4 4PH. **Tel.** Bedale (677) 60235. **Telex** No. **Owner** John Sharp. **Open** March–Dec. **Rooms** 8 double with bathroom (1 including hand shower) and tea-making facilities. No phone or TV in rooms. **Facilities** 2 reception rooms, 1 with TV, dining room, 8-acre gardens and grounds. Fishing by arrangement. **Restrictions** Dogs not to be left unattended in bedrooms. **Terms** Moderate. Special 2-day-break rates, Nov., March and April (not Easter). **Credit cards** None. **Getting there** M1 to A1 for Thirsk, B6267 to Masham, A6108 (Middleham direction) for 5 miles. About 5 hrs. **Helicopter landing** Yes (2 days notice). **Of local interest** Dales, Richmond; Fountains Abbey, Newby Hall. **Whole day expeditions** Castle Howard, York; Ripon. **Refreshments** White Dog, Howgrave. **Dining out** Black Bull, Moulton.

Aristocratic splendor near ancient York

Historic House Hotels is an organization which buys lovely old country houses, restores them, and opens them as luxurious country house hotels. Middle-thorpe Hall, built about 1700 by a wealthy master cutler, and sometime home of the wildly eccentric traveller and diarist Lady Mary Wortley Montagu, needed months of work before it was ready to receive guests. Eight layers of paint had to be stripped from the panelling of the Oak Dining Room and parts of the magnificent woodwork of the wide staircases were expertly recarved. The black-and-white marble hall and intricate plasterwork of the ceilings took weeks to refurbish. Splendid bathrooms were installed, with the sort of solidly good-quality marble and chrome usually found only in the better European hotels. Each has an efficient shower as well as a tub. Décor was supervised by Mrs Robin Compton, whose own stately home, nearby Newby Hall, has won awards for its inspired restoration.

However, it is the quality of the welcome and care of the guests that ultimately is most important. Malcolm Broadbent, formerly of the superb Stafford Hotel in London's St James's, has brought his French wife and family to York, and is now Middlethorpe Hall's General Manager and host. Under his keen professional eye everything runs smoothly, and he is always about, greeting new arrivals, circulating in the restaurant, ready to answer enquiries or give touring advice. When I entered the elegant front hall on a cold evening, a log fire burning brightly in the hearth was instantly welcoming, and there was a liveried hall porter to carry in my luggage. My room was delightful; it had antiques, a pomander to hang among the clothes, and a supremely comfortable bed which was turned down for me at night. The walls seemed to be covered with dark plum-colored suede, but proved to have been cleverly painted.

Drinks are served in the vast drawing room, where guests can study the dinner menu and the wide-ranging wine-list, which includes some excellent vintages. The restaurant is in three adjoining rooms, where white damask cloths, polished silver, and delicate flower arrangements in fine porcelain vases complement the talented and imaginative cooking. Duck and orange soup, delicately flavored, turbot with wild mushrooms, freshest of fresh vegetables, a melon sorbet, and home-made truffles with coffee were all perfect.

Outside, the grounds are fast regaining their past splendor, and the ancient stable block has become especially luxurious extra bedrooms. The nearby ancient walled city of York has a history of Romans and Vikings, ghosts and legends. Its maze of narrow medieval streets encircle the towering Minster, and are packed with enticing shops and marvellous museums. Middlethorpe Hall provides the supremely comfortable base for sightseeing.

Opposite: A grand hotel both inside and out. Above: dinner is a fine display of china and silver. Overleaf: left, looking into the walled garden; right, two of the hotel's splendid interiors.

MIDDLETHORPE HALL, Bishopthorpe Road, York, North Yorkshire YO2 1QP. **Tel.** York (0904) 641241. **Telex** 57802, A/B MIDDLE G. **Owners** Historic House Hotels. General Manager, Malcolm Broadbent. **Open** All year. **Rooms** 31 (5 suites, 18 double, 5 single, 1 four-poster, 2 twin), all with bathrooms (including wall showers), color TV, direct-dial phone, radio. **Facilities** Hall, drawing room, library, upstairs sitting room, dining in three separate rooms, downstairs grillroom, conference/dining room, lift, laundry/dry cleaning, 26-acre gardens with lake, croquet lawn. **Restrictions** No dogs; children over 8 welcome. **Credit cards** All major cards. **Terms** Medium (2-day Champagne Break 1 Nov.–31 March). **Getting there** M1, A1, A64 to Bishopthorpe, just s of York. About 4 hrs. 2 hrs by rail – hotel chauffeur can meet trains. **Of local interest** York; Castle Howard; Selby. **Whole day expeditions** Newby Hall; Ripon; Fountains Abbey; Rievaulx Abbey; Whitby; Robin Hood's Bay; Yorkshire Moors. **Refreshments** Star, Harome; Ebor, Bishopthorpe. **Dining out** Pool Court, Pool-in-Wharfedale.

Gracious hospitality in a sumptuous setting

I must confess to a partiality for Rookery Hall. Appearing unannounced one Saturday for lunch, I found myself the only guest, all others having departed to some function. Instead of being waited on with glum faces by a staff who otherwise would have had a welcome rest, I was greeted with enthusiasm, served an excellent lunch, and made to feel that the one concern of the chef and his numerous assistants was that I should enjoy my meal. A subsequent stay did not disillusion me.

Rookery Hall is a vast mansion, and its grounds include a stable block, a walled garden, a lake, and parkland with ancient oak trees. Alterations by its second owner, Baron von Schröder, in the mid-1800s gave it the imposing European look it has today. Candlelight throws into relief coats-of-arms in the fine plasterwork of the ceiling of the larger dining room; the smaller has 18th-century panelling rescued from a demolished mansion. Both look out over lawns, flower borders, and a fountain to unspoilt countryside. The enormous drawing rooms, imposing staircase, and formally dressed staff could be intimidating, but are not, since everyone is friendly, courteous, and helpful. Mr and Mrs Peter Marks, who only recently became owners of this their first hotel, lived for ten years in Monte Carlo, had a holiday home in Arizona, and travelled widely. They have been able to apply their experience as guests to the organization of comfort for others. When you arrive at Rookery Hall the Marks will probably be in the hall to greet you. Staff instantly appear to carry up bags and produce a teatray with gleaming silver and china so fine it has to be handwashed. A waiting letter greets you, suggests dinner arrangements, and encourages you to ask for anything you need. Since a bowl of fruit, freshly baked cookies, high quality

toiletries, and helpful touring information are already provided you are wondering what else you could possibly need when a small bottle of excellent champagne is brought up in a silver ice bucket, compliments of the management. This VIP treatment is accorded to all.

Master chef Clive Howe presides over the magnificent new kitchens. Dinner began with marinated breasts of quail, sautéed in butter, served warm with a salad of courgette and apple in a light vinaigrette. River salmon in chicory and dill sauce was followed by a water-ice of Lamberhurst wine, loin of local lamb, home-made pasta and fresh vegetables. Farmhouse cheeses, sultana bread and a hot lemon soufflé with raspberry sauce and fresh cream concluded a superb meal. Staying at Rookery Hall is a most gracious experience.

Opposite: the hotel rises from trim lawns. Above: tea arrives in a silver service. Overleaf: left, the dining room and an exquisitely arranged salad; right, a rococo stove carries a bust of Michelangelo's "David."

ROOKERY HALL, Worleston, Near Nantwich, Cheshire, CW5 6DQ. **Tel.** Nantwich (0270) 626866. **Telex** 367169 ATT ROOKHALL. **Owners** Peter and Audrey Marks. **Open** All year. **Rooms** 2 suites, 7 double, 2 singles, all with bathroom (including wall or hand shower), color TV, direct-dial phone, radio. **Facilities** 2 public dining rooms, 1 private dining room, 2 salons, 28-acre grounds and gardens, tennis court, croquet, putting, coarse fishing in River Weaver, clay-pigeon shooting. Riding nearby. **Restrictions** No children under 10, no dogs, no smoking in dining room, jacket and tie at dinner. **Terms** Expensive. Special breaks, special Christmas program. **Credit cards** All major cards. **Getting there** M1, M6, Junction 16, A500 to Nantwich, A52/51 (still to Nantwich). Across rail crossing, then at traffic circle take A51 towards Chester, through 2 sets of lights, R on B5074 to Winsford. Hotel 1½ miles on R. About 3 hrs (15 mins. from M6). **Helicopter landing** Yes. **Of local interest** Wedgwood pottery; Chester. **Whole day expeditions** Peak District; North Wales. **Refreshments and Dining out** Nothing nearby.

Designer living

Hambleton Hall was built for house-parties. The motto above the door, "Fay ce que voudras" ("Do as you please"), reflects the philosophy of its original owner, a wealthy young bachelor. Refusing to go into the family business, he built this mansion to entertain the Prince of Wales' set – lively young people who escaped the stiff court etiquette and disapproving beady eye of Queen Victoria whenever possible. The house-party tradition continued into the 1920s; Noël Coward was staying here when he wrote *Hay Fever*.

Overlooking Rutland Water, and reached by a narrow peninsular of land that juts into the lake, Hambleton Hall has a solid Victorian stateliness. It is at the end of a curving drive, sheltered by huge cedars; terraces of flowers and shrubs lead down to parkland and the lakeside. The atmosphere of the house is one of calm sophistication. Merchant banker Tim Hart and his wife, Stefa, with the famous interior designer Nina Campbell, have created a series of beautiful and striking rooms. "Fern" is white and cool, with leafy green and dark blue touches. "Qazvin" is exotically eastern, in dark red and orange, with a four-poster bed. Wallpapers, fabrics, furniture (both antique and modern), handwoven bedcovers, bedlinen, doorplates, china (individually designed for each room), and flowers are brought together in a *tour de force* of design. Several of the staff were formerly with London's Connaught Hotel.

Sitting in a comfortable chair by the fire, I sipped my nicely chilled dry sherry and munched miniature savoury crab and smoked salmon delicacies while studying the menu. The dining room, newly redecorated and resplendent, was elegant, formal but friendly, and the food was of the highest quality. Fine pastry leaves were filled with Dublin Bay prawns in a saffron mayonnaise. A grilled cutlet of halibut was

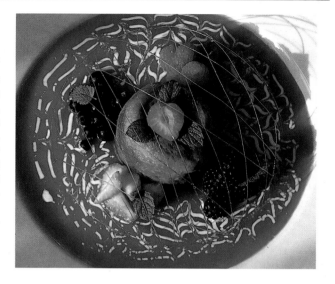

sharpened by a touch of bitter orange; crisply roasted duck, served with tiny vegetables, was mellowed by the delicate sweetness of blueberries. There was an excellent cheeseboard, and all the staff were impressively well-informed about the merits of each cheese. I found some delicious Brillat-Savarin, and followed it with a brandysnap basket filled with a Grand Marnier mousse, fresh strawberries and raspberries, topped with a golden coronet of spun sugar. Succulent petits-fours accompanied excellent coffee. Upstairs, Malvern water and freshly made shortbread waited beside a neatly turned-down bed. I left feeling that I had been visiting wealthy country acquaintances with impeccable taste and perfect manners.

Opposite: the entrance bears the pleasure-lover's motto, "Do as you please." Above: a beautifully presented summer pudding. Overleaf: left, the impressive garden front and a luxurious bedroom; right, the hotel's view over Rutland Water.

HAMBLETON HALL, Hambleton, Oakham, Leicestershire, LE15 8TH. **Tel.** Oakham (0572) 56991. **Telex** 342888 A/B HAMBLE G. **Owners** Tim and Stefa Hart. **Open** All year. **Rooms** 15 double, all with bathroom, color TV, radio and direct-dial phone. **Facilities** Drawing room, dining room, bar, private dining room, lift, 17-acre grounds, hard tennis court. Pheasant shooting, horse riding, fishing, fox hunting (in season) and golf, by arrangement. **Restrictions** Children under 5 and dogs, by prior arrangement with management. No dogs in public rooms, or left unattended in bedrooms. **Terms** Expensive. Special discount break (3 nights or more) of 50% off double room, available Nov.–April, excluding Saturdays, Easter and Christmas. **Credit cards** All major cards. **Getting there** A1 to Stamford, A606 direction Oakham. 1 mile before reaching Oakham, turn L to Hambleton/Egleton village only. About 2½ hrs. **Helicopter landing** Yes (24 hrs notice). **Of local interest** Stamford; Burghley House; Belton House; Althorp House; Belvoir Castle. **Whole day expeditions** Lincoln; Ely; Cambridge. **Refreshments** White Horse, Empingham; Noel Arms, Whitwell; Ram Jam Inn, Stretton. **Dining out** Whipper-Inn, Oakham.

Old English ways with New World ideas

Gerald Milsom, ebullient and enthusiastic, shares with Francis Coulson and Brian Sack of Sharrow Bay (see p. 13) the distinction of being one of England's longest established hoteliers. Like them, he began by running a tea-shop, Le Talbooth, a charming ancient riverside house which today is his gourmet restaurant. Inspired by visits to America he has gone on to build a "mix-and-match" hotel and restaurant empire, where guests have plenty of choice, and can sign as they go, receiving just one final bill at the end of their stay. He has been joined by sons David and Paul, who bring the latest in modern expertise to organizing these five establishments.

The Dedham Vale Hotel was run by Gerald's parents as a family hotel until they were in their mid-eighties. When he took over, he added the splendidly exuberant Edwardian-style conservatory restaurant, plant-hung and yellow-draped, where I enjoyed a delicious home-made leek soup from a big pot, and the wide selection of cold dishes from the buffet. In the evenings there is a rotisserie and grill, as well as an alternative menu of spicy Indian dishes created and constantly supervised by TV chef Rafi Fernandez. The large bar is decorated with fenland scenes and *trompe l'oeil* perspectives by a pupil of Annigoni, Lincoln Taber, who also decorated the Gazebo Lounge at the Savoy in London. A bar and a comfortable sitting room look out onto the lovely 2-acre wooded grounds, and over smooth lawns and bright flowers, floodlit at night. The bedrooms have simple, cottage-style décor, with flowery matching wallpaper and bedcovers, plain, well-equipped bathrooms, and velvet easy chairs.

Half-an-hour away by car is another Milsom establishment, The Pier, a fish restaurant in the deepwater port of Harwich. The big Scandinavia-bound ferries pass startlingly close to its windows, but no longer tie up alongside as in Victorian times, when Harwich was the Great Eastern railway terminus. The restaurant in this charming period building serves the grander fish dishes upstairs – lobster, Dover sole, smoked salmon – and downstairs more down-to-earth fish and chips and fish snacks. There are plans to add a few simple bedrooms. In the heart of the nearby ancient city of Colchester is a café, The Pavilion on the Square, which is the latest addition to this string of hotels and restaurants.

Throughout his establishments Gerald Milsom has revitalized Old English ways with New World ideas, providing delightful rural retreats only an hour-and-a-half from London.

Glimpsed through tranquil greenery – the hotel in its riverside setting (opposite). Above is the cool, airy, plant-hung conservatory restaurant.

DEDHAM VALE HOTEL, Stratford Road, Dedham, Colchester, Essex CO7 6HW. **Tel.** Colchester (0206) 322273. **Telex** 987083 LETALB G. **Owner** Gerald Milsom OBE. **Open** All year. **Rooms** 6 double, all with bathroom (no showers), radio, color TV, direct-dial phone. **Facilities** Lounge, bar, restaurant, 3-acre grounds, 100 yards from river. **Restrictions** No dogs. **Terms** Moderate. **Credit cards** All major cards. **Getting there** A12, turn off after Colchester for Stratford St Mary and Dedham. Hotel down hill on L. About 1½ hrs. **Helicopter landing** Yes. **Of local interest** Constable country; Flatford Mill; villages of Kersey and Nayland; half-timbered market town of Lavenham; Long Melford; Colchester. **Whole day expeditions** Cambridge; Newmarket; Bury St Edmunds; Ely; Norwich; Norfolk coast. **Refreshments** Woolpack and Fleece, Coggeshall; Marlborough Head, Dedham; House without a Name, Easthorpe; Fort St George, Cambridge; Ferryboat (with ghost), Holywell, Nr Cambridge. **Dining out** Hintlesham Hall; Le Talbooth, Dedham.

Live in style in Constable country

Much favored by film stars and diplomats passing through London, Maison Talbooth is in the heart of the gentle countryside made famous in the early 19th century by the paintings of John Constable and remarkably unchanged since.

Undergrowth has recently been cleared away in the gardens of the Maison Talbooth, to open up the fine views over fields and woodland. A big round fountain, floodlit at night, now stands before the house, encircled by the gravel drive, and there is a giant chess set with outsize pieces set in the lawn near the French windows. The plain, color-washed exterior of the hotel gives no hint of the opulence of its large, luxurious bedrooms, lavishly draped and individually furnished, which are named for English Romantic poets. Each has an ornate bed or beds, an enormous and elaborate mirrored bathroom — some with a large round sunken bath in a raised dais — plenty of closet space, direct-dial phone, color television, a mini-bar, and comfortable chairs and settees. There is no impression of staying in a hotel. You arrive, sign the guest book, the friendly and helpful staff settle you into your room, and vanish. You may then wander at will in the grounds, or relax in the big soft chairs in the drawing room before the fire, undisturbed. You have only, however, to lift the phone for instant service.

Breakfast arrives in your room in the mornings, elegantly presented. There is, at the moment, no restaurant at the Maison Talbooth, but there are plans to add a conservatory restaurant serving elegant light snacks: smoked salmon, patés, salads, and coffee. Visitors have a choice of restaurants and menus, however, since the owner of Maison Talbooth, Gerald Milsom, owns two establishments nearby, the Dedham Vale Hotel, with a lunchtime

cold buffet, evening rotisserie, and alternative Indian menu (see p.33), and Le Talbooth, a lovely 1520s half-timbered building on the banks of the River Stour, one of Constable's favorite subjects. Here gourmet French and traditional British dishes are served by candlelight at polished tables bright with fresh flowers and silver. There is an excellent and skilfully-chosen wine list.

East Anglia is a much underrated part of England. Its churches, huge and elegant, dwarf the little villages huddling round them, and were built with the wealth of the medieval wool trade. Look up into the darkness of their wooden rafters: the beam-ends often carry flights of serene angels with outstretched gilded wings. Many great families have their ancestral homes here, near the Queen's own royal estate at Sandringham. With racing at Newmarket, and the ancient university city of Cambridge close by, there is much to tempt visitors, whose explorations will be enhanced by the thought of the luxuries of the Maison Talbooth awaiting their return.

Elegant French windows lead into the grounds from the comfortable drawing room (opposite). One of Maison Talbooth's sumptuous bathrooms is pictured above — a lavish contrast to the old-world exterior of Le Talbooth (overleaf, top right). The grand, close-carpeted bedrooms (overleaf, bottom right) are luxuriously furnished.

MAISON TALBOOTH, Stratford Road, Dedham, Colchester, Essex CO7 6HN. **Tel.** Colchester (0206) 322367. **Telex** 987083 LE TALB G. **Owner** Gerald Milsom OBE. **Open** All year. **Rooms** 1 suite, 9 double, all with bath (no shower), direct-dial phone, color TV, radio, minibar. 5 rooms on ground floor, baby listening. **Facilities** Drawing room, 3-acre grounds with fountain, giant chess, croquet. **Restrictions** No dogs. **Terms** Expensive. **Credit cards** All major cards. **Getting there** A12, exit after Colchester at turning marked Stratford St Mary and Dedham, follow Dedham signs, hotel on R after about ¾ mile. About 1½ hrs. **Helicopter landing** Yes. **Of local interest** Constable country; Flatford Mill; villages of Kersey and Nayland; half-timbered market town of Lavenham; Long Melford; Colchester. **Whole day expeditions** Cambridge; Newmarket; Bury St Edmunds; Ely; Norwich; coast. **Refreshments** Woolpack and Fleece, Coggeshall; Marlborough Head, Dedham; House without a Name, Easthorpe; Fort St George, Cambridge; Ferryboat (with ghost), Hollywell, Nr Cambridge. **Dining out** Hintlesham Hall.

1920s elegance in a glorious garden

When Jeremy Mort, who already had hotel experience, and Allan Holland, successful entrepreneur and inspired, self-taught gourmet cook, first saw Mallory Court, a twenties mansion in its own ten-acre estate, they knew at once that this was the somewhere special they had been looking for. Although the house had always been a family home, they firmly believed that a building designed for a gracious life-style and frequent house parties must work marvellously as a hotel. Without feasibility studies or market research, they plunged into the mammoth task of restoring the neglected rooms and overgrown gardens of this lovely country estate to their original glory. First, they refurbished the front part of the house, and opened it as a restaurant. The delicious food produced by Allan, working initially in somewhat primitive conditions in the original kitchen, and the delightful and attentive service supervised by Jeremy in the oak-panelled dining room with its cool green linen napery, proved an instant success. They were then able, room by room, to restore the fine woodwork, original bathrooms, spacious reception rooms, and large bedrooms. Finally they turned their attention to the terraces, rose garden, water garden, squash court, swimming pool, and orchard. When they added anything, such as extra bathrooms, they used fittings of the same high quality as the originals.

Mallory Court is now immaculate. The lovingly tended, exquisitely orderly gardens are glowing with color. Inside the house, everything is polished and shining, and the staff are delighted to see you when you arrive. Bedrooms and bathrooms are provided with every thoughtful detail. The one suite has not only a large balcony overlooking garden and beautiful countryside, but also an enormous bathroom with two bathtubs and a tall, free-standing, plate-glass shower stall. The cosseted guests, having relaxed with television or one of the many interesting books, and thumbed through the comprehensive touring information provided, come down to comfortable chairs, freshly-baked small delicacies served with pre-dinner drinks, and the contemplation of a tempting menu. I tried the crustacean consommé (light and appetizing), asparagus in featherlight pastry with a slightly orange-flavored hollandaise (different and nice), quail with fresh grapes (juicy and tender), and a perfect raspberry soufflé. Hand-made chocolates followed with the coffee; the wine-list was of high quality. The whole atmosphere was peaceful and relaxing. The personality of the owners does not intrude: Jeremy Mort is almost always there, but is quiet and self-effacing. All I saw of Allan Holland was his tall white chef's hat and starched jacket gleaming in the distance as he gathered herbs and garnishings in the early morning from the superb kitchen garden. Mallory Court is a place to which my thoughts, when I am busy, bothered, or harrassed, turn longingly back.

Opposite: Coffee in an elegant setting. Above: a welcoming bedroom. Overleaf: left, the hotel at night; right, a view of the gardens and a glimpse into one of the stylish bathrooms.

MALLORY COURT, Harbury Lane, Tachbrook Mallory, Nr Bishops Tachbrook, Leamington Spa, Warwickshire CV33 9QB. **Tel.** Leamington Spa (0926) 30214. **Telex** 317294 MALORY G. **Owners** Jeremy Mort and Allan Holland. **Open** All year. **Rooms** 1 suite, 8 double, all with bathroom, 5 with showers (3 wall mounted), phone, radio, color TV. 1 with four-poster bed. **Facilities** Lounge, drawing room, dining room, sun-lounge, 10-acre grounds, water garden, rose garden, terraces, outdoor swimming pool, squash court, all-weather tennis court, croquet, golf 2 miles away. **Restrictions** No children under 12, no dogs.

Terms Medium. 3-day breaks available, 1 Nov.–end March. **Credit cards** Access/Amex/Visa/Diners. **Getting there** M1, at exit 16, A452 from Leamington Spa; after 2 miles, turn L towards Harbury. Hotel about 100 yards on R. About 2½ hrs. **Helicopter landing** Yes (24 hrs notice). **Of local interest** Royal Leamington Spa; Stratford-upon-Avon; Warwick; north Cotswolds; gardens at Hidcote. **Whole day expeditions** Oxford; Gloucester; Blenheim Palace; Cheltenham. **Refreshments** Sir Toby's, Stratford-upon-Avon; Smithy's, Warwick. **Dining out** Grafton Manor, Bromsgrove.

A family home rich in historic associations

Hidden away amid leafy countryside, at the end of a long and now well-surfaced lane, Grafton Manor is a fascinating house with an intriguing history, which has an excellent restaurant, and is run by a delightful family, John and June Morris and their grown-up children.

The Manor is noted in the Doomsday Book as belonging to a nephew of William the Conqueror; the present house was erected in 1567 as the principal seat of the Earls of Shrewsbury, though part of it was rebuilt after a disastrous fire in the 1700s. Conspirators in the Gunpowder Plot of 1605 are known to have stayed here before leaving for their ill-fated mission to London. They probably met upstairs in the Great Parlor, where there is a vast crested overmantel, which together with the huge entrance porch survived the fire untouched. In the evenings, drinks and exceptionally delicious canapés are served here. The restaurant, awarded three red crossed knives and forks and a red M from Michelin – high praise indeed – is downstairs.

Dinner was highly enjoyable. Carrot and coriander soup was served in a large tureen which was left on the table for further sampling; the bread was warm and home-made. A sea- and shell-fish soufflé flan was light and delicate, trimmed with a sprig of chervil and fennel and a purple borage flower. A complete, tiny pigeon-pudding had a rich sauce and an accompaniment of perfect vegetables. Home-made sorbets, hand-made chocolates, and excellent coffee completed a perfectly seasoned, delectable meal. The wine-list is notable for some exceptional Burgundies. I retired to sit luxuriously before the twirly cast-iron grate of the gas coal fire in my bedroom.

The family themselves, and not a decorator, have restored the bedrooms one by one with ingenuity and

charm, making light-fittings, hunting out large-patterned papers to suit the high-ceilinged rooms, and choosing rich fabrics which have been expertly sewn by a local lady. Bathrooms are luxurious. Outside is a giant herb garden (once a cricket pitch), divided into big squares. The house has its own chapel, tithe barn and a big walled garden which the Morrises hope to restore. There is a medieval "fish stew," or holding-pond, for fish from the two-acre lake, and an ancient ruined dovecot whose fate is alas uncertain, because of the large investment required to restore its full splendour. There is a distant prospect of the motorway.

When you arrive, the family is so welcoming that you feel like a relative coming home – which is, after all, how a family-run hotel should feel.

Opposite: the red-brick exterior is dominated by the 16th-century porch. Below: the food is as elegantly arranged as the checkerboard herb garden. Above: one of the comfortable bedrooms.

GRAFTON MANOR, Grafton Lane, Bromsgrove, Hereford and Worcester B61 7HA. **Tel.** Bromsgrove (0527) 31525 or 37247. **Telex** No. **Owners** John and June Morris. **Open** All year. **Rooms** 1 suite, 6 double, 1 single (more in preparation), all with bathroom including shower (2 wall-mounted), color TV, direct-dial phone, gas/coal fire. **Facilities** Great Parlor, 2 dining rooms (conference room in preparation), 25-acre grounds, 2-acre lake with coarse fishing, croquet. Golf nearby. **Restrictions** No dogs in hotel (kennels provided). No children under 5 in restaurant, under 7 in hotel. **Terms** Medium. **Credit cards** All major cards. **Getting there** M1, M6/M42 to Exit 1, signposted Bromsgrove. Turn L (s) for Bromsgrove on B4091. After about $2\frac{1}{2}$ miles turn right at 4th set of traffic lights, turn R on Hanbury Road for $\frac{1}{4}$ mile, turn R at T-junction on B4091. 100 yards to Grafton Lane, on L. About $2\frac{1}{2}$ hrs. **Helicopter landing** Yes. **Of local interest** Avoncroft Museum of Buildings; Worcester; Royal Brierly crystal factory; Stratford-upon-Avon; Warwick. **Whole day expeditions** Welsh border castles; Ludlow; north Cotswolds. **Refreshments** Eagle and Sun, Droitwich. **Dining out** Mallory Court, Bishops Tachbrook (see p.39).

Six centuries of history, lovingly restored

Shortly after the Doomsday Book was written, the owner of the estate on which Flitwick (pronounced "Flittick") Manor now stands replaced the old wooden Saxon village church with one in stone. Though much altered, the same church is still there today, on its knoll beside the Manor, overlooking woods, lake, and fields. The house is an attractive mixture of styles and periods – Elizabethan, Georgian, Victorian – with a stableyard and walled garden whose bricks are time-weathered to a rich terracotta shade. A few miles from the M1, midway between Oxford and Cambridge, it is surrounded by an urban sprawl which gives one pause, but Flitwick needs only to be glimpsed to reassure.

The drive leads up through an avenue of limes, the ground beneath them carpeted with snowdrops and bluebells in the spring, to a garden full of fine specimen trees, and a view over unspoilt countryside. There is a small, busy entrance hall with an ancient open fire and a graceful curving staircase. The panelled bar has an antique zinc-topped Austrian sideboard, an elaborate cast-iron grate, and a collection of china sardine dishes. There is also a small sitting room and a Gothic Drawing Room. Interesting antiques, model ships, prints, paintings, and bric-à-brac are scattered throughout. A large wooden chest on the landing is full of green wellington boots, which guests are encouraged to borrow for wandering through the 50-acre grounds. My bedroom, in the oldest part of the house, had a low, beamed ceiling and rattan furniture. A tempting bowl of fruit with plate, knife, and napkin, accompanied a most comprehensive drinks tray with ice and sliced lemons. Plenty of books and magazines, Scrabble, and playing cards were also provided, and the bathroom had everything from a spare toothbrush to a wooden sailing boat for the bath tub.

Owner Somerset Moore and his French wife, Hélène, previously ran a most successful award-winning restaurant. Since Flitwick is especially noted for its seafood, I ordered the excellent crab and mussel soup, flavored with saffron and cream, followed by a generous dish of fresh shellfish, including succulent crayfish, shrimps, prawns, and a large oyster. The salad and frothy lemon dessert were good and there were home-made truffles with the coffee.

Flitwick Manor has changed hands for money only three times: in 1361, in 1632, and at the end of the 1970s; otherwise it has been passed down from one generation to another by inheritance. Lovingly restored and beautifully decorated, in the hands of Somerset and Hélène Moore it has become a memorable hotel, and a most satisfactory base from which to tour the Cotswolds or East Anglia.

A footnote: Flitwick Manor is haunted, but only on Christmas Day, which is why it closes for Christmas.

Charming old-English style characterizes Flitwick indoors and out. Above: pretty floral chintzes adorn a four-poster bed – clearly a home-from-home for one resident!

FLITWICK MANOR, Church Road, Flitwick, Bedfordshire MK45 1AE. **Tel.** Flitwick (0525) 712242.**Telex** 825562 FM. **Owners**Somerset and Hélène Moore.**Open** All year. Closed 25/26 Dec. Restaurant closed Sunday nights to non-residents.**Rooms** 2 suites, 12 double, 3 single, all with bathroom (2 including shower), direct-dial phone, color TV, radio, minibar. 3 bedrooms are on the ground floor. **Facilities** Hall, small sitting room, drawing room, dining room, library/bar, 50-acre gardens and grounds, including 3-acre lake, tennis, fishing, putting, croquet, bicycles, snooker, table-tennis. Golf, sailing, windsurfing, badminton, squash nearby by arrangement. **Restrictions** No dogs in public rooms.**Terms** Medium. Half-price night Fri. and/or Sun. if Sat. booked. **Credit cards** All major cards.**Getting there** M1, Exit 12 (Ampthill road), hotel on L after 3 miles, just before Flitwick. About 1 hr.**Of local interest** Woburn; Luton Hoo; Hatfield House. **Whole day expeditions** Cotswolds; Oxford; Cambridge; London; Windsor; Thames Valley. **Refreshments and Dining out** Paris House, Woburn.

A tranquil rural retreat

The name "Hope End" does not signify despair, but has the old English local meaning "a place at the end of a hidden valley," which exactly describes this unique house. The huge estate surrounding it, in the lovely Malvern Hills, was owned by Elizabeth Barrett Browning's father in the early 1800s. He built for his wife and eleven children a vast Moorish extravaganza of a house with minarets, extending (and dwarfing) the original modest Queen Anne building. It was Elizabeth's home for twenty-three years of her early life, before the family moved to Wimpole Street in London – from which she eloped with poet Robert Browning. A later owner demolished much of the fantastic structure, leaving just one lone minaret, a huge archway, iron gates, some stables, and the little red-brick Queen Anne house. These were inherited by Patricia Hegarty, a teacher. With her lawyer husband, John, she has transformed them into a most intriguing family home and country hotel.

The Hegartys are serious but kind and their delightful house is immaculate. Natural wood, sealed but not painted, is used everywhere, even in bathrooms. There are two enormous black wood-burning stoves to sit round in the evenings although even on the coldest of days the house itself is beautifully warm. There are books everywhere. The peace of the valley, the enormous trees, the grassy slopes leading down to a lake largely taken over by bullrushes and wild mallards, the smell of wood smoke, the neatness and harmony of colors in the house, and the faint aroma of delicious food in the making reminded me of a New England house deep in the woods or a Swiss mountain cabin. One bedroom is in a cottage totally removed from the house, surrounded by trees, birds, and rabbits, and evokes delight – or alarm – at its solitude.

Patricia Hegarty cooks only locally produced meat, fish, and game, and uses fruit from her own trees, vegetables from her own walled kitchen garden. The lentil soup had smoky overtones from good ham stock, the brown bread was freshly baked and the lamb was accompanied by vegetables picked just before cooking. It was followed by a mixed salad, fresh local cheese, an egg custard with a swirl of caramel and heavy cream, and a selection of either coffee or exotic teas. The good wine-list has a wide range of half-bottles. There is no choice on the menu, but it changes for every meal. Pure Malvern water – so thoughtfully provided in bottles by many hotels – here is on tap from springs in the local hills.

House martins nest under the eaves; bantams wander in the yard; rural, tranquil, and quietly excellent, this is every city-dweller's dream of escape.

Opposite: a peaceful country setting – and a minaret! Below is a beautiful display of the local produce that goes into Patricia Hegarty's cooking. Above: one of the harmoniously decorated rooms.

HOPE END COUNTRY HOUSE HOTEL, Hope End, Ledbury, Hereford and Worcester HR8 1JQ. **Tel.** Ledbury (0531) 3613. **Telex** No. **Owners** John and Patricia Hegarty. **Open** Last weekend in Feb. to last weekend in Nov. NB closed every Mon. and Tues. **Rooms** 9 double, 7 in house, 1 under minaret across courtyard, 1 in cottage. All with bathroom, phone (not direct-dial); only the cottage has TV and direct-dial phone. **Facilities** 3 sitting rooms, 1 dining room, 40-acre grounds including parkland, bluebell woods, lake, walled garden. **Restrictions** No dogs, no children, no smoking in dining room. **Terms** Moderate. Bookings of 2 or more nights preferred. Reductions for longer stays. **Credit cards** Visa/Access. **Getting there** M40/A40 to Cheltenham via Oxford. M5 to Exit 9 (Tewkesbury), A438 to Ledbury, B4214 under railway bridge, turn R to Wellington Heath, after about 2 miles bear R. Hotel on L. About 2½ hrs. **Helicopter landing** No. **Of local interest** Malvern Hills and Three Choirs music festival (August); walks; National Trust and other gardens; Tewkesbury. **Whole day expeditions** Cheltenham; Gloucester; Ludlow; Hay-on-Wye (antiquarian book shops); Wye Valley; Border castles; Offa's Dyke footpath; Welsh mountains. **Refreshments** Cottage of Content, Carey; Fleece, Bretforton; Butcher's Arms, Woolhope. **Dining out** Croque-en-Bouche, Malvern; Walnut Tree, Abergavenny. (NB terms at Hope End include dinner).

Cotswold comforts in a medieval manor

Buckland Manor is exactly what comes to mind if one imagines an ancient manor house in the Cotswolds: a rambling, picturesque, honey-colored stone building close by the tower of the village church. Buckland is an enchanting place, secluded and quiet, although only two miles from the famously beautiful village of Broadway, with its many craft and antique shops but, alas, over-plentiful summer visitors.

Adrienne and Barry Berman found the 13th-century Manor in excellent condition when in 1982 they created a comfortable hotel from what until then had always been a private house, without loss of atmosphere or charm. The bedrooms have soft, fitted carpets, direct-dial telephones and color televisions; all have exceptionally luxurious bathrooms – some also have excellent showers (so rare in England). There is a gracious dining room, hung with historic portraits in oils, which has pleasant country views by day and at night is softly lit by many candles. It was added to the Manor at the beginning of this century, when many of the rooms were panelled in dark oak.

This is a place in which to relax and be pampered. The Bermans are most anxious that their guests should enjoy their stay, and spare no pains to ensure their comfort.

Visitors mid-tour may be relieved to find that their menu is not only a fine example of calligraphy, but is also entirely *à la carte*, giving freedom of choice, unlike the sometimes overwhelming succession of set courses that may be offered in other country house hotels. *Bavarois de légumes Arc-en-ciel* was both colorful and delicious, as was a *granité* of red wine. Turbot interlaced with smoked salmon was served with a shallot and butter sauce and a generous

quantity of tiny fresh vegetables. Home-baked bread served with the meal is plentiful and delicious, as are the desserts and the excellent selection of cheeses. Service by the young staff was obliging and dinner was leisurely, as it must be when everything is cooked to order. One particularly pleasing touch I noted is that soup arrives in big tureens which are left on the tables for guests to dip into at will.

Behind the Manor, well tended gardens rise up the hillside to a series of terraces, with rose beds, arbors, and walks. Beyond is a little stream bordered by water-loving plants and an uncultivated area where wild orchids and snake's-head fritillaries grow.

Buckland Manor is quiet and rural, yet luxurious and sophisticated, and is ideally placed for exploring the many delights of the Cotswolds, for visiting Stratford-upon-Avon or Cheltenham, or for pausing en route to Scotland or the north of England.

Opposite: roses in bloom in the well-kept gardens. Above: four-poster comfort. Overleaf: luxury, superb food, and a glorious Cotswolds setting.

BUCKLAND MANOR, Buckland, Nr Broadway, Gloucestershire W12 7LY. **Tel.** Broadway (0386) 852626. **Telex** No. **Owners** Barry and Adrienne Berman. **Open** All year (except 3½ weeks from mid-Jan.). **Rooms** 11 double, all with bathroom, 3 have shower as well as tub. Direct-dial phones, color TV, radio on request. 2 four-poster beds, some ground-floor rooms. **Facilities** 2 sitting rooms, writing room, dining room, 10-acre grounds, gardens, heated pool, tennis court, croquet lawn, putting green. **Restrictions** No children under 12; dogs in kennels only; no pipes or cigars in restaurant. **Terms** Expensive. Some winter and special event all-inclusive terms. **Credit cards** Access/Visa. **Getting there** M40 to Oxford, A40 to Burford, A424 to Broadway via Stow-on-the-Wold. In Broadway L on B4632 (signposted Cheltenham), L again after 1½ miles (signposted Buckland). 1¾–2 hrs. **Helicopter landing** Yes (24 hrs notice). **Of local interest** Cheltenham; Stratford-upon-Avon; Cotswolds market towns and villages; antique and local crafts shops, riding, golf; gardens at Hidcote, Kiftsgate, Sezincote, and Barnsley House; Warwick Castle. **Whole day expeditions** Oxford; Woodstock; Bath; Broughton Castle. **Refreshments** Black Horse, Naunton. **Dining out** Mallory Court, Bishops Tachbrook (see p.39).

A luxury inn at the gates of Blenheim Palace

When research into local records failed to produce an inspiring name for his new hotel, Gordon Campbell-Gray thought of his much-prized collection of stuffed birds and decided upon "The Feathers." A jay ornaments the reception desk; there are seagulls on the stairs, snowy owls and a buzzard in the bar. In other nooks and crannies of the four 17th-century houses which form this fascinating hotel there are also books, china, prints, paintings, potted plants, more birds, and beautifully arranged vases of flowers pleasantly complementing attractive furniture. A pair of solid wooden 18th-century Spanish cartwheels are used as occasional tables in the bar. There are four meandering stairways and a network of interconnected passages. The stone-flagged reception area was once a butcher's shop; the grander section at the side, which has a tall archway and gates, was the home of local dignitaries; the restaurant had humble beginnings as a teashop.

Mr Campbell-Gray previously helped to run an enormous and extremely elegant château in Holland as a hotel. Turning to something completely different he bought and transformed The Feathers. Everything that gives the houses character has been lovingly preserved; everything shoddy, shabby, or unsightly has been stripped away. Bricked-up fireplaces have been opened and are in use, even in some bedrooms. Hand-hewn beams, ancient stonework, antique pine panelling mellowed by time to a rich honey color all show the skills of craftsmen in the past, which is why Mr Campbell-Gray prefers to have hand-made furniture repaired and re-upholstered rather than to buy factory-made reproductions. Each bedroom is different; all are delightful. The subtly lit restaurant has a sophistication usually found in Manhattan or Rome; the menu

unusually and pleasingly offers to simplify any dish to the customer's taste. The excellent game pâté with Cumberland sauce, fillets of plaice wrapped round fresh salmon mousse, carrots with orange zest, spinach with mushrooms, cream, and nutmeg, and the strawberry and passion fruit sorbets were all light and delicious.

Woodstock is a charming town, full of shops selling antiques, china, handicraft, and silver. It is at the very gates of Blenheim Palace, home of the Duke of Marlborough and birthplace of Sir Winston Churchill. Local people drop into The Feathers for a traditional tea, family Sunday lunch, or for special celebrations; international travellers find a comfortable home from home.

Opposite: the old-world charm of the entrance, and one of the interiors – as beautifully designed as the food (above).

THE FEATHERS HOTEL, Market Street, Woodstock, Oxfordshire OX7 1SX. **Tel.** Woodstock (0993) 812291. **Telex** 83138 TELKAY G. **Owner** Gordon Campbell-Gray. **Open** All year. **Rooms** 14 double, 2 single, all with bathroom (5 with shower, 2 without tub), color TV, direct-dial phone. **Facilities** 2 dining rooms (1 private), garden bar, panelled parlor, drawing room, small garden. (NB all meals provided, including Sunday lunch and afternoon tea.) **Restrictions** Dogs by arrangement only. **Terms** Moderate (include full breakfast). 2-night all-inclusive winter breaks available.

Credit cards All major cards. **Getting there** A40/M40 to Oxford, turn R at ring road, A34 to Woodstock. About 1½ hrs. **Helicopter landing** No. **Of local interest** Blenheim Palace and grounds; Woodstock; Oxford; Cotswolds; Warwick Castle; Stratford-upon-Avon; Broughton Castle. **Whole day expeditions** London; Gloucester; Cheltenham. **Refreshments** Trout, Godstow; Falkland Arms, Great Tew; Bear and Ragged Staff, Cumnor. **Dining out** Le Manoir aux Quat' Saisons, Great Milton (see p.55); Le Petit Blanc, Oxford.

The splendid country house of a master chef

Raymond and Jenny Blanc took a daring step when they moved from their modest Oxford premises to a lovely, mainly 18th-century manor house several miles outside the city, but when the Michelin Guide transferred its seldom-awarded two-star rating to the new establishment even before it opened to the public – an almost unheard-of mark of confidence in the chef – success seemed assured.

Great Milton is a pretty village with thatched cottages, a village green, and several stately stone houses scattered about its periphery. Turn through the attractive gates that have been adopted as the hotel's symbol and the lovely façade of the Manoir appears, decorated with bright flowers and surrounded by picturesque outbuildings, including a very handsome dovecot. On sunny days the small lawn to the right of the Manoir sports bright pink umbrellas under which guests sip cooling drinks. On the left is a heated pool and beyond that is the village church, in which can be found fragments of the early 14th-century tomb of the Manoir's first owner, a Frenchman – like the present owner and many of the restaurant staff. Twenty-seven acres of gardens, fields, and woods ensure peaceful surroundings. Flowers are everywhere: they bloom profusely in the garden and appear in exceptionally elegant arrangements in reception rooms and corridors. There are modest pink and white nosegays on the pink linen cloths in the restaurant. Each bedroom is named for a flower, with which it is decorated in season. I stayed in "Bluebell," a pretty attic room with dormer windows and leaded lights. The enormous bathroom had thick soft towelling wraps, a huge oval bath and French soap, shampoo, and foam bath. The fitted carpet was the misty blue of a bluebell wood in spring, the walls were palest green and the bedcover

and curtains were of crisp white glazed cotton faintly patterned with bluebells.

The exquisite décor forms the setting for the superb cuisine. A scallop terrine with baby leeks looked almost Japanese in its decoration and symmetry. A domed silver cover was lifted to reveal slices of meltingly tender lamb fillet, fanned into a central rosette and wreathed with minute, perfect, baby vegetables from the extensive kitchen garden. A lemon soufflé was a captive breath of air, perfumed with lemon, dusted faintly with sugar, vanishing instantly in the mouth. Coffee, as expected, was excellent and it was hard to choose from the selection of luxury French wines (there are good regional specialities). Next morning's breakfast, brought to my bedroom on a huge silver tray was equally superb. Service is impeccable – attentive, swift, and elegant, but never condescending. Raymond Blanc provides gracious surroundings for those who come to sample his culinary expertise and outstanding food for those who come just to relax.

Opposite: the dignified manor house basks in the sun. Above: looking into the moat. Overleaf: great comfort, magnificent food, and beautiful gardens are everybody's memory of Le Manoir.

LE MANOIR AUX QUAT'SAISONS, Great Milton, Oxfordshire OX9 7PD. **Tel.** Great Milton (084 46) 8881. **Telex** 837552 BLANC G. **Owners** Raymond and Jenny Blanc. **Open** All year, except 24 Dec.–20 Jan. Restaurant closed all day Mon. and Tues. (light lunch for residents). **Rooms** 10 double, all with bathroom, including hand showers, 2 with separate showers, color TV, radio, direct-dial phone. **Facilities** 3 dining rooms (1 private), reception hall, drawing room, sitting room, heated outdoor pool, hard tennis court, riding stable, 27-acre grounds with water-gardens and carp fishing. **Restrictions** No children under 8; dogs in kennels in grounds only. No smoking in restaurant. **Terms** Very expensive. Mid-week reductions. **Credit cards** All major cards. **Getting there** A40/M40, Exit 7. Turn L for Great Milton 8 miles before Oxford. Hotel 2 miles on R. About 40 mins. **Helicopter landing** Yes (24 hrs notice). **Of local interest** Oxford; Cotswolds. **Whole day expeditions** Stratford-upon-Avon; Woodstock; Blenheim; Windsor. **Refreshments** Trout, Godstow. **Dining out** Le Petit Blanc, Oxford.

Home is a castle with royal connections

Thornbury is everything that a castle should be. It has battlements and towers looking towards the Welsh hills. There are turrets and tall twisting Tudor brick chimneys and inscribed on its gatehouse and overmantels are the coat of arms and badges of the ancestors of the Dukes of Buckingham. Henry VIII spent ten of his thousand days with Anne Boleyn here, and Mary Tudor lived here for some years before becoming queen. Of recent times, a lovely garden has been planted within the outer walls, and a vineyard laid out in the ancient base-court, where in the Middle Ages cattle and castle retainers lived. Luxurious bedrooms have been created, and the castle has become an impressive hotel and a perfect centre for touring the Cotswolds, Bath, and the Welsh borders.

You might imagine that it would be impossible to make a castle comfortable, but that is what has been done. Corridors are carpeted and well-lit. Bedrooms have high ceilings and tall mullioned windows with warmly lined curtains, plenty of space for clothes and luggage, thoroughly modern bathrooms, many extra small luxuries, and, in several cases, impressive four-poster beds. The main suites are stupendous: the upper room in the octagonal tower has an almost oriental canopy of deep rose brocade over its four-poster, an open hearth, and a bathroom with gold-plated fittings. Before dinner guests study the menu and magnificent wine-list in the Old Library, which looks out over the clipped yew hedges and flower borders to the tower of the village church beyond. Sorrel soup, venison and cherry pie in its own little dish with a perfect crust, delicious fresh vegetables, and damson icecream were excellent, well presented, and charmingly served by staff who are as international as the clientèle.

The Castle's new owners, Maurice and Carol Taylor, have taken over chef and staff, and maintained the traditions established over twenty years by Kenneth Bell, who opened Thornbury as a celebrated restaurant and later added bedrooms for visitors. They hope to restore more of the rooms, continuing the long but extremely exciting task of bringing all of the castle back to life. They have already re-opened one of the huge fireplaces, which cheers what was a rather dark room, and added many more fresh flowers, and some very fine antiques, paintings and tapestries. Thornbury Castle's future seems assured, in such good hands.

Opposite: heraldic glass in the dining room. Above: garden chairs under the battlements. Overleaf: the atmosphere of a medieval castle lingers on – although Henry VIII never slept in so comfortable a four-poster!

THORNBURY CASTLE, Thornbury, Bristol, Avon BS12 1HH. **Tel.** Thornbury (0454) 418511. **Telex** 449986 CASTLE G. **Owners** Maurice and Carol Taylor. **Open** All year except Christmas. **Rooms** 12 double, 2 single, all with bathrooms (no showers), color TV, radio, direct-dial phone; 1 on ground floor, 4 with four-posters. **Facilities** Lounge, library, 2 dining rooms, 15-acre grounds and gardens with vineyard, croquet. Ballooning, golf, shooting by arrangement. Hotel car and chauffeur available for expeditions.

Restrictions No pets. No children under 12. No smoking in dining rooms. **Terms** Medium. Winterbreak packages. **Credit cards** All major cards. **Getting there** M4 to exit 20. On A38 N towards Gloucester. After 4 miles, turn L onto B4061 for Thornbury. About 2½ hrs. **Helicopter landing** Yes (24 hrs notice). **Of local interest** Bristol; Cotswolds. **Whole day expeditions** Bath; Stratford-upon-Avon. **Refreshments and Dining out** Many places locally – ask hotel.

Invitingly snug

As I walked through the front door of Esseborne Manor, a cheerful bearded gentleman shot out of the kitchen, still in his cook's striped apron, with his feet comfortably clad in carpet slippers. He greeted me warmly, carried my bags upstairs, and offered me a surprisingly wide selection of teas and coffees. The jasmine tea of my choice was brought swiftly to the small comfortable sitting room where I was already browsing through a book. Although it was a chilly gray day just before Christmas, the house was beautifully warm and my bedroom invitingly snug. Everything I could possibly want was provided, including plenty of big towels in the bathroom and a yellow duck for the bathtub. A folder on the dressing table contained offers to wash and iron clothes (or lend board and iron), find stamps for letters, or clean shoes left outside my door at night. I was exhorted to request anything lacking. I felt cosseted, and looked forward optimistically to dinner.

The menu was short and hand-written, almost always a good sign, and the well-explained wine list featured not only better-known wines but also excellent vintages from the same regions as the great vineyards, produced at more sensible prices. My delicious chicken liver salad had a light dressing, and included white grapes and just-cooked crumbled crunchy bacon. A small glass of sharp grapefruit sorbet followed, then a perfect partridge, stuffed with raisins, hazelnuts, and celery, the rich sauce flavored with a hint of orange. Fresh cabbage, tiny green beans, and potatoes with a touch of nutmeg were all just right. There was preserved ginger and crisp meringue mixed into my coffee icecream, served with caramel sauce. The cheeses, all British, were in perfect condition and the petits-fours with the coffee were splendid. All this, it transpired, had been cooked by the charming girl who was only the hotel team's *reserve* cook.

Esseborne Manor's age is difficult to guess, since it was much altered in Victorian times. It is built on lands granted by Henry III in 1216 to an order of nuns who owned the estate for the next 300 years. Bought by a group of friends, one a former hotel inspector, it has been lovingly restored, the gardens replanted to include a big herb garden, and the tennis court resurfaced. A paved patio with a fountain separates the manor from a new building with larger and more sophisticated bedrooms. Do not come here if you are looking for a very grand country house with enormous rooms and hovering staff. Staying at Esseborne Manor is like visiting kind and indulgent friends who cook very well and are extremely helpful, but do not fuss.

Bright and welcoming with evening floodlights (opposite, above), Esseborne's sturdy stone walls contain delightful English décor and design (opposite, below and above).

ESSEBORNE MANOR, Hurstbourne Tarrant, Andover, Hampshire SP11 OER. **Tel.** Hurstbourne Tarrant (026 476) 444. **Telex** No. **Owners** Peter Birnie, Philip Harris. **Open** All year, except 2 weeks over Christmas. **Rooms** 12 double (those in second building larger), with bathroom (including wall shower), color TV, direct-dial phone, radio. **Facilities** Sitting room, bar, dining room, large garden, croquet, tennis, golf practise net. **Restrictions** No pets, no children under 10. **Terms** Moderate. Special all-year 2-day discounts. **Credit cards** All major cards. **Getting there** M4, exit Newbury, A343 off Newbury ringroad. Hotel on L after $7\frac{1}{2}$ miles. About $1\frac{1}{2}$ hrs. **Helicopter landing** Yes, by arrangement. **Of local interest** Mottisfont Abbey; Broadlands; Avebury; Winchester; Salisbury; Stonehenge; motor racing at Thruxton; horse racing at Newbury; Watermill Theatre at Newbury. **Whole day expeditions** Bath, Oxford, New Forest. **Refreshments and Dining out** Nothing nearby.

A centuries-old tradition of hospitality

The village of Hunstrete (once "Houndstreet") is first mentioned in AD 936. Hunstrete House itself was built in the 18th century, of golden stone which time has weathered to gray. A square, stately building, in wooded grounds, approached up a long drive that curves gently through the deer park, it is at first sight so imposing as to be slightly intimidating. This impression is quickly dispelled by the friendly warmth of the greeting by the staff. The comfortable chairs, huge arrangements of flowers from the garden, magazines and books scattered about, and the fires which are rapidly kindled in the many fireplaces if the day turns chilly, evoke an atmosphere of home rather than hotel. The owner, John Dupays, supervises the care of the magnificent gardens, and his wife, Thea, has collected the many antiques and chosen the lovely fabrics that make each of the large, well-furnished bedrooms individual and charming. Each bedroom is named after a native British bird, with a framed print of that bird on the wall: I was intrigued to find myself staying in "Pipit." Seven of the rooms are in a converted stable block, which is reached by crossing a charming courtyard almost Mediterranean in atmosphere, with a fountain and many cheerful flowers. The rooms in the annexe are as spacious and luxurious as those in the main building.

The standard of the cooking matches the comfort of the house. Robert Elsmore, the prize-winning chef, delights in the wide variety of fresh fruit and vegetables grown in the hotel's own extensive kitchen gardens and orchards. The taste of vegetables and herbs picked in the morning to go straight into the pot is vastly different from that of produce bought in markets. As well as the delicate sauces and featherlight pastry accompanying his delicious venison, red mullet, succulent pink lamb, and exotic puddings, for which he has always been justly famous, he is proud of the fact that all the bread and croissants for breakfast, and the scones and cakes for tea, are baked in his kitchens each day. Bacon is from a local farm, eggs are from the hotel's own free-ranging hens, and the delicious selection of jams and conserves is made from their own fruit. It must be pointed out, I feel, that the venison on the menu comes from Scotland, and not from the deer grazing round the house! The broad-based wine-list features some exceptional wines, and is compiled with evident expertise.

The welcoming hospitality offered to guests at Hunstrete House maintains a long tradition stretching back to medieval times, when a monastery stood on the site and entertained weary pilgrims on their way to the miraculous shrine at Glastonbury Abbey.

Opposite and above: gray walls and glowing interiors make an intriguing contrast. Overleaf: left, sun catches the fountain's horses; right, warmth and style are combined in the rooms.

HUNSTRETE HOUSE, Hunstrete, Chelwood, Nr Bristol, Avon BS19 4NS. **Tel.** Compton Dando (076 18) 578. **Telex** 449540 HUNHSE. **Owners** John and Thea Dupays. **Open** All year, except early Jan. **Rooms** 20 double (including 1 suite), 1 single (3 more rooms in preparation), all with bathrooms including showers (2 wall-mounted), direct-dial phone, color TV and radio. 4 bedrooms are on the ground floor. **Facilities** Drawing room, library, bar, 3 dining rooms (smoking and non-smoking, and private), 90-acre grounds, heated outdoor swimming pool, hard tennis court, croquet lawn, coarse fishing. **Restrictions** No dogs, children over 9 only, no smoking in Terrace Dining Room.

Terms Very expensive. Special 3-day breaks, early Nov.–end March. **Credit cards** All major cards. **Getting there** M4 to exit 18, A46 to Bath, A4 through Bath towards Bristol for 4 miles, A39/A368 for Wells and Weston-super-Mare, hotel 1 mile after Marksbury. **Helicopter landing** Yes (by arrangement). **Of local interest** Bath; Wells; Stourhead Gardens; Lacock; Montacute House; Wilton House; Glastonbury. **Whole day expeditions** The Cotswolds; Exmoor; Thomas Hardy country; Wales and the Wye Valley; Salisbury Plain. **Refreshments** Carpenters Arms, Stanton Wick. **Dining out** Homewood Park, Hinton Charterhouse (see p.73).

In the grand style

What do you do when you inherit from your family many very beautiful, very large, very much loved pieces of 18th-century furniture? The answer, in the case of Peter and Christine Smedley, is that you buy a magnificent 18th-century mansion from the editor of the London *Times*, restore it to its original palatial grandeur, using the best materials and finest craftsmanship, add marble bathrooms and warm central heating, an elegant restaurant, and a staff of friendly local girls in neat uniforms, and open it as a superb country hotel.

Ston Easton is also the Smedleys' home, complete with an amiable spaniel and family portraits in the yellow dining room. Each room is individually charming: the lofty Palladian Saloon; the panelled restaurant in the Tudor core of the house; the enormous bedrooms with lofty four-posters; the smaller bedrooms tucked under the eaves, each with antiques, delightful fabrics, and well-chosen items of china or cut glass, silver, or embroidery. The chef uses only the finest and most fresh ingredients and his food is beautifully presented on delicate white Wedgwood china.

The house was the property of one family for over four hundred years. On the death of the last of the line, the contents were sold, and demolition threatened. Vandals stole the lead from the roof, so that the lovely, gracefully curving staircase to the right of the hall became a rushing torrent every time it rained. Rescued by a preservation order, the house was eventually bought by the Smedleys. Some of the original fixtures never left, or have been returned. The library book-shelves were sold to the USA, but an export license was refused; kitchenware, sold for pennies to someone in the village, will now form part of an exhibition when the original basement kitchens are restored. The 1770 portrait of the household servants by Thomas Beech, sold in 1956, has recently been willed back to the house by its buyer, and hangs again in the yellow dining room. This shows the housekeeper, who is supposed to have murdered the little stillroom maid (also portrayed) for love of the bailiff, one of the two male servants in the picture. It is the maid who still, it is said, haunts the upper floors of the house, quietly walking about, opening and shutting doors, never seen, never malevolent, but very much there. She is undisturbed by the restoration of the twenty bedrooms.

The Smedleys, totally undaunted by their Herculean task, have put the finishing touches to the rooms, which are impeccably maintained, and are now replanting the gardens to the plans drawn up by Humphry Repton, the famous landscape designer, in 1792. At a time when so many great country houses are in decay, Ston Easton has taken on a glorious new lease of life.

Opposite and above: every detail of these magnificent rooms repays attention. Overleaf: the stately exterior and antique-filled interiors are immaculately maintained.

STON EASTON PARK, Ston Easton, Nr Bath, Avon BA3 4DF. **Tel.** Chewton Mendip (076 121) 631. **Telex** 444738 AVOSTL. **Owners** Peter and Christine Smedley. **Open** All year. **Rooms** 20, incl. 11 twin, 1 single, 1 double, 6 four-posters, 1 suite, all with bathroom (most with wall showers), color TV, radio, and direct-dial phone. **Facilities** Hall, Saloon, drawing room, library, 2 dining rooms, private yellow dining room, billiard room. Croquet, ballooning by arrangement, river, 25-acre parklands. **Restrictions** No children under 12, no dogs in public rooms or bedrooms, free kennelling in basement. **Terms** Expensive. 2-night winter breaks (Nov.–end March, not Christmas, Easter or Fridays). **Credit cards** All major cards. **Getting there** M4, Exit 18, A46 to Bath, A39, A37 to Ston Easton. About 2 hrs. **Helicopter landing** Yes (same day). **Of local interest** Bath; Bristol; Wells; Bradford-on-Avon; Glastonbury; Cheddar Gorge; Mendip Hills; Lacock. **Whole day expeditions** Stonehenge; Avebury; Stourhead Gardens. Information sheet available. **Refreshments** King's Head, Litton; Carpenter's Arms, Chelwood. **Dining out** Popjoys, Bath; Homewood Park (see p.73); Hunstrete House (see p.65).

Homewood Park

Hinton Charterhouse
Avon

Good cooking and a relaxed atmosphere

A private country house until bought by Stephen and Penny Ross, Homewood Park was built mainly between the mid-18th and mid-19th centuries, although its cellars are much older. Stephen and Penny, busy with their Bath restaurant, Popjoys, had never meant to run a hotel, but when they saw the house they knew they had to buy it. They have already won back the garden, which has an arboretum and flourishing herbaceous borders, and have increased the number of bedrooms to fifteen: they feel this is the maximum to which they can give good personal attention while not neglecting their young family.

I was sure that I was going to enjoy my stay at Homewood Park even before I saw it, because the letters and telephone calls exchanged during booking had been so welcoming. Drawing up in front of the curiously ancient porch (filched, perhaps, by some previous owner from the Abbey ruins nearby), I was hardly out of my car before a cheerful girl appeared, knowing exactly whom to expect, and organized a young man to carry up my bags. This was just as well, for my room was at the very top of the house. The reward for climbing all the stairs, pausing from time to time to examine the attractive pictures, was the spectacular view from the dormer window over lovely rolling countryside. It was a most appealing room. A six-feet-wide double bed on a low dais had a canopy which followed the slope of the ceiling and a bedhead of matching cushions suspended from a brass rod. The pale orange, yellow, and pink of its delightful honeysuckle-pattern fabric were echoed in the colors of the wallpaper. Pale apple-green wall-to-wall carpeting set everything off pleasingly. The bathroom was also a delight, in solid golden modern oak, with plenty of surfaces for toiletries. It had cheerful green plants, a shower boosted by a pump for good pressure, and a tub backed by white tiles embossed with a raised pattern of fruit. Scattered throughout the house are bronzes by a family friend, David Backhouse, which may be purchased.

Dinner was excellent: spinach soup with freshly baked bread faintly flavored with rosemary was followed by venison with redcurrants, braised lettuce, new potatoes, and firm courgettes, and a wonderful chocolate soufflé. The quality of the wine-list will be much appreciated by connoisseurs. The young staff are enthusiastic, dedicated, and friendly and there is a feeling of welcoming informality about the place that is particularly attractive. A frequent comment I heard was "Homewood Park is not as formal and grand as some places near Bath, but I really *like* it!"

Opposite and above: the gardens at Homewood Park are as lovely as the charming interiors.

HOMEWOOD PARK HOTEL, Hinton Charterhouse, Bath, Avon BA3 6BB. **Tel.** Limpley Stoke (022 122) 3731 and 2643. **Telex** 4444937 HOMWOD G. **Owners** Stephen and Penny Ross. **Open** All year, except 24 Dec.–7 Jan. **Rooms** 15 double, all with bathroom (with wall shower), 2 dining rooms, conference room, 10-acre grounds, tennis court, arboretum. Golf and clay pigeon shooting nearby, indoor/outdoor country club sporting facilities 1 mile away, by arrangement. **Restrictions** No dogs in hotel building. No smoking in dining room. **Credit cards** All major cards.

Terms Medium. **Getting there** M4, off at Exit 18 to Bath, from which take A36 (Warminster road) for $5\frac{1}{2}$ miles. Turn L (signposted Sharpstone). Hotel is first L turning. About $2\frac{1}{2}$ hours. **Helicopter landing** Yes (2 days notice). **Of local interest** Bath, Stonehenge, Avebury, Marlborough, Salisbury. **Whole day expeditions** Hardy's Dorset, Mendip Hills and Wells. **Refreshments** The Wheatsheaf, Combe Hay; The Hop Hole, Limpney Stoke. **Dining out** Hunstrete House, Hunstrete (see p.65).

Gourmet dining in an old-world hotel

Visitors arriving in Taunton in late spring will probably find The Castle Hotel smothered in wisteria blossom. It is an oasis of quiet in the center of a busy town, and faces a wide square. The remains of its Norman moat and keep are now a charming garden with flowering cherry trees, spring bulbs, and a green lawn. Once inside its thick walls, you could be in the heart of the country. The history of the castle goes back over twelve hundred years, and it has seen crowned heads passing through since Anglo-Saxon times. It became a hotel some three hundred years ago. From the first it was a notable hostelry and stage-coach stop. It has continued to entertain royalty, including Queen Victoria and the present Queen Mother.

From the moment that your bags are taken by a uniformed hall porter, you are looked after with professional efficiency and West Country charm. Managing Director Christopher Chapman is no newcomer to the hotel business. His grandfather managed the London Savoy in its Edwardian heyday: the legendary parties he organized there before being tempted to New York by a salary "larger than the Prime Minister's" are still remembered with awe. Christopher Chapman's father and mother began the process of modernizing The Castle which he has continued, still with their help. The very comfortable bedrooms are not only well designed, but have splendid bathrooms with efficient showers. Each room has a different décor, some using antiques, velvets, and brocades, others chintz, wicker, and bamboo. One tower room has a tall arched bedhead which echoes its arched window. The barman in the welcoming Rose Room is swift and efficient, and not only remembers which drink you ordered last time, but also your name and room number. The restaurant is elegantly formal, with a high ceiling, tall windows, and chandeliers.

Both traditional and gourmet menus are offered by the young British chef, Gary Rhodes, who arrived via distinguished French establishments and London's Capital Hotel. I enjoyed a well-seasoned consommé containing plump ravioli of bresaola and pink shallots, a light mousseline of sea bass, wrapped in salmon, with a delicate lemon and chervil butter sauce and a garnish of asparagus tips, excellent new potatoes, broccoli and green beans, and an orange soufflé daringly punctured on serving to pour in a Grand Marnier cream. Coffee and hand-made chocolates followed. It is a pleasure to stay in a good hotel, impeccably maintained, with a caring staff, in an interesting city, and then to find also that they have a memorable chef.

Opposite and above: neat flower gardens in the Norman moat, four-poster beds, and afternoon tea in this especially welcoming hotel.

THE CASTLE HOTEL, Castle Green, Taunton, Somerset TA1 1NF. **Tel.** Taunton (0823) 272671. **Telex** 46488 A/B CASTLE G. **Owners** The Chapman family. Managing Director, Christopher Chapman. **Open** All year. **Rooms** 35, incl. 1 large suite, and 4 smaller suites, all with bathroom (tub and shower), radio, color TV, direct-dial phone. **Facilities** Lift, Rose Room with bar, Oak Room, restaurant, 1½-acre grounds with garden (incl. Norman well). **Restrictions** Dogs by arrangement only and not in public rooms. **Terms** Medium. **Credit cards** All major cards. **Getting there** M4, M5, Exit 25 to center of Taunton. About 2¾ hrs. **Helicopter landing** Yes (2 days notice). **Of local interest** Exmoor and Lorna Doone country, Dorset and Thomas Hardy country, King Arthur's Glastonbury, Wells, Stourhead. Hotel provides excellent touring information and maps. **Whole day expeditions** Thorough exploration of one of the above! **Refreshments and Dining out** There are many small local places; the hotel will provide suggestions.

Far from the madding crowd

If you arrive at Boscundle Manor during the afternoon, you may find Mary Flint happily weeding her beloved garden. She will not be in the least discomposed at being surprised in her gardening clothes, and will cheerfully summon her husband, Andrew, who will help with your bags, settle you into your room, and prepare a welcoming cup of tea. Anybody who has recently been staying at very formal establishments may find this unnerving, but they need be in no doubt about the comfort of the simple bedrooms, or the excellence of the meals served in the dining room, which gleams with polished mahogany and shining silverware.

Andrew Flint, impeccably besuited, orchestrates swift and efficient service, is highly knowledgeable about wines, and has compiled an excellent and very reasonable wine-list. He is justly proud of the delicious Stilton soup, sole Véronique, duckling with cherry and brandy sauce, traditional desserts with Cornish clotted cream, and other expertly prepared dishes, which have won high praise for Mary from Michelin Inspectors as well as from local gourmets. Andrew himself is no novice in the kitchen – he cooks all the breakfasts.

The Flints are escapees from a fast-track London life. Andrew had a senior post with an internationally famous group of city chartered accountants; Mary used to help run a prestigious secretarial agency. Visiting Cornwall, they saw and fell in love with Boscundle Manor and its garden, then a wilderness. They do not know a great deal about the history of the house, except that the very thick walls of the cottage that was the original building on the site suggest medieval origins. Part of the Manor is probably Georgian, and the whole building rambles about in the haphazard way of houses that have been added to over the centuries. A pleasant small bar has been built at the rear, and a conservatory-breakfast room at the side. The Flints have filled their home with an intriguing assortment of antiques. Paintings by their friend Fred Yates have been hung throughout; his charming Cornish scenes (rather in the style of L. S. Lowry) are in many important collections worldwide and may be purchased here. The garden is the Flints' great passion, and as well as planting many trees, shrubs, and flowers, they have also constructed a swimming pool, terrace, and summerhouse. With their own hands they moved massive granite blocks to form flights of steps and levelled terraces, and they have also laid out a croquet lawn. They have recently bought another cottage on which they are working. Enthusiastic, indefatigable, and welcoming hosts, it is hard to believe, after having spent only an evening with them, that one has not known them for years.

Opposite and above: Boscundle Manor has an atmosphere of rural peace both inside and out.

BOSCUNDLE MANOR, Tregrehan, St Austell, Cornwall PL25 3RL. **Tel.** Par (072 681) 3557. **Telex** No. **Owners** Andrew and Mary Flint. **Open** All year, except end Oct.–early March. Restaurant closed to *non*-residents Sunday and lunchtime. **Rooms** 9 double, 2 single, 6 with bathroom (5 including shower), direct-dial phone, color TV, radio. 2 suites and 2 cottages also available. **Facilities** Drawing room, bar, restaurant, conservatory, 2-acre hillside garden, $7\frac{1}{2}$ acres of adjoining woodland (with old tin mine), croquet, heated outdoor pool, 3 golf practice holes, tennis. **Restrictions** No dogs in public rooms. **Terms** Moderate.

Credit cards Visa/Amex/Access. **Getting there** M4 to Bristol, M5 to Exeter, A38 to Dobwalls, A390 to St Austell. About 5 hrs. **Helicopter landing** Yes. **Of local interest** Fowey, Megavissey, and Roseland peninsula. Coastal path walks. Many Celtic remains; many local artists. Cothele estate, Lanhydrock, Trewithin, and Trelissick gardens. **Whole day expeditions** Bodmin Moor (Jamaica Inn at Bolventor); St Ives; Zenor; Cape Cornwall; St Michael's Mount. **Refreshments** Pandora Inn, Mylor Bridge; Roseland Inn, Philleigh; Crown, St Ewe. **Dining out** Food for Thought, Fowey; The Fish Restaurant, Padstow.

Michelin-starred cuisine on the edge of Dartmoor

It is a curious fact that one of England's most delightful and characteristically English country house hotels is run by Americans. Paul and Kay Henderson have made Gidleigh Park what it is today, not in a few months of multi-million restoration and designer revamping, but by years of dedicated and loving hard work. They have now brought house and garden to a peak of perfection and have tempted down to their remote edge-of-Dartmoor setting a tremendously talented chef, Shaun Hill, who shares their enthusiasm for moorland rambles. As a result, Kay has finally been able to abandon her cooking pots and pans and join Paul in solicitously overseeing the comfort of their guests.

Gidleigh Park is set into a hillside with splendid views and magnificent terraced gardens leading down to a river which hurries tumultuously over large rocks. There are smooth green lawns and opulent flower beds, including great banks of rhododendrons through which views to the moors have been cleared. The house's spacious hall and public rooms are panelled in oak, with wide hearths and a faint, sweet smell of wood-smoke. Siamese cats stretch sinuously before the fires, and greet visitors with distant courtesy. The staff are more warmly welcoming and the beautifully furnished bedrooms provide all one could wish, including books, excellent bathrooms, and towelling robes. Some rooms are vast, some are tucked up cosily under the eaves, two others a few yards away are in what was formerly the chapel, and those at the front have especially amazing views.

Paul Henderson has endeared himself to the English by his fierce love of Dartmoor, his determination to turn a rambling mansion into a luxurious and relaxed home, and his sang-froid, which is displayed by his decision to stay open all the year round, although most West Country hotels close

for winter. He has been proved right, for people come regardless of the season. What has charmed visiting Americans is the friendly yet very sophisticated atmosphere and the magnificent cuisine. On the evening I was there, Shaun Hill cooked a superb meal, and when he emerged from his kitchen he proved to be sparkling company as well.

The setting, the ambience, and the Michelin-starred cooking all make this an exceptional hotel. Paul told me that although it is one of the most expensive country house hotels in England, he believes it is also one of the best. A daring claim when people often have to make a very long journey to reach the hotel, but I am happy to say that in my opinion he is absolutely right.

Opposite: sunlight glittering on the river below Gidleigh Park, the perfect setting for a tasteful, quintessentially English retreat (above).

GIDLEIGH PARK, Chagford, Devon TQ13 8HH. **Tel.** Chagford (06473) 2367. **Telex** 42643 GIDLEY G. **Owners** Paul and Kay Henderson. **Open** All year. **Rooms** 14 double, all with bathrooms (8 with shower), direct-dial phone, color TV, radio. **Facilities** Hall, drawing room, bar, 2 dining rooms, terrace, extensive garden with river, tennis, croquet, walking, fishing. Riding, golf nearby. **Restrictions** No dogs in public rooms. **Terms** Very expensive. 3- and 7-day winter breaks, Nov.–March.

Credit cards All major cards. **Getting there** M4/M5/A30 to Whiddon Down. Follow signs for Chagford (not Gidleigh). In Chagford, R at Lloyds bank, 1st fork R, look out for hotel sign, about 2 miles. About 4 hrs. **Helicopter landing** Yes. **Of local interest** Dartmoor National Park; Exeter; Castle Drogo. **Whole day expeditions** Cothele and Lanhydrock Houses; N and S Devon coasts. **Refreshments** Tea at Primrose Cottage, Lustleigh. **Dining out** Carved Angel, Dartmouth (1½ hrs).

Explore Thomas Hardy's native county

This is the perfect place to stay for devotees of Thomas Hardy's novels who wish to explore his Dorset, or visit his birthplace at Higher Brockhampton, or walk on "Egdon" (Winfrith) Heath, or stay in Sturminster Newton, where he wrote *The Return of the Native*; it is also ideal for those who wish to climb the immense ramparts of Maiden Castle, built four thousand years ago, or buy handthrown bowls from Bernard Leach's grandson at Muchelney Pottery, or stand in Wareham's tiny Saxon church of St Martin in front of the effigy of Lawrence of Arabia slumbering in Arab robes, head on a camel saddle.

Prideaux-Brunes have lived at Plumber Manor for over three hundred years. Their portraits hang in an upstairs gallery in the square Jacobean house. Richard Prideaux-Brune, Old Harrovian and A Character, will welcome you in the stone-floored entrance hall, which has a graceful staircase, accumulated family bric-à-brac (including a stuffed Greenland falcon), and bowls of fresh flowers. He will be on hand later to serve you drinks from the well-stocked bar in the sitting room. The delightful restaurant, favored by the local gentry, is presided over by the chef, his brother Brian, who produces reliably delicious food from a reassuringly short menu based on daily deliveries of fresh produce. Crab with melon, loin of pork with calvados, cream, and apple, and almond meringue with brandy and apricot sauce were excellent. It was hard to decide between the mouth-watering selection on the dessert-trolley, all prepared daily on the premises. The bedrooms in the main house are comfortable and convenient, those in the stable block larger and yet more splendid to compensate for the minor inconvenience of walking the few yards to the main house (golf umbrellas provided). As Richard Prideaux-Brune says, "This is

all part of our house, and we would not want, or put up with, shoddy workmanship."

As well as strolling in the 300-acre estate, keen gardeners will enjoy a visit to nearby Stourhead, probably England's finest landscape garden, or to Montacute House, which has a splendid formal Elizabethan garden stocked with strains of traditional roses. On the coast not far away is Lyme Regis, whose lovely surroundings and chalk cliffs are the haunt of fossil hunters. Scenes in Jane Austen's *Persuasion* and John Fowles's *The French Lieutenant's Woman* are set here.

Plumber Manor is not there to cosset and indulge its guests. It provides an excellent dinner, a comfortable bed, a hearty English breakfast and advice, if required, about what to see. After this guests set off for the day to explore Dorset, returning in the evening to the Prideaux-Brune family waiting to hear of the day's exploits.

Opposite and above: the discreet driveway leads to a country gentleman's attractive home.

PLUMBER MANOR, Sturminster Newton, Dorset, DT10 2AF. **Tel.** Sturminster Newton (0258) 72507. **Telex** No. **Owner** Richard Prideaux-Brune. **Open** All year, except Feb. Restaurant sometimes closed to non-residents Sun./Mon. evenings Nov.–March. **Rooms** 12 double, with bathroom (with wall shower), color TV, direct-dial phone. **Facilities** Sitting room/bar, drawing room, 3 dining rooms, 300-acre estate, croquet, hard tennis court. **Restrictions** No dogs, no children under 12. **Terms** Moderate. Full breakfast included. 2- or 3-day winter breaks Oct.–April (not Christmas and Easter). **Credit cards** Visa/Access. **Getting there** M3/A30 signposted Salisbury. In Salisbury, A354 to Blandford Forum. Turn R onto the A357 for Sturminster Newton. Just beyond village turn L at Red Lion pub, for Hazlebury Bryan. Hotel $1\frac{1}{4}$ miles on L. About $2\frac{1}{2}$ hrs. **Helicopter landing** Yes. **Of local interest** Valley of River Piddle; Montacute; Stourhead. **Whole day expeditions** Salisbury. **Refreshments** Brace of Pheasants, Plush; Fiddleford Inn, Fiddleford. **Dining out** Stock Hill House, Gillingham.

Sophisticated splendors

The New Forest – new that is for William the Conqueror – was a royal hunting preserve, ruthlessly formed by flattening several Saxon villages, driving off the inhabitants, and imposing savage penalties on trespassers. For disturbing the deer, blinding; for shooting arrows at the deer, a hand cut off; for killing a deer, death. The site of Chewton Glen Hotel was by then already inhabited. Happily the laws governing the area are no longer so brutal, though many medieval forestry regulations still survive. The present house on the site was owned in the mid-19th century by the brother of Captain Marryat, author of *The Children of the New Forest*, who spent some time here, and from whose books the names of many of the rooms are taken. Chewton Glen is now a world-famous hotel, as sophisticated and in tune with the life of the international traveller as any of the better London hotels, and yet it has not lost the friendly and welcoming atmosphere of a gracious private house in the country. Bedrooms are sunny and elegantly chintzy, designed for comfort and furnished with taste, and all possessing that (for England) rare delight, a thermostatically controlled shower. Many bedrooms have balconies. The suites in the old stable are on two floors, and have a tiny garden and an extra bathroom each. The view over the main gardens is of smooth green lawns, stone urns overflowing with colorful cascades of flowers, neat gravel walks, a terraced pool, and a backdrop of trees. Downstairs, François Rossi presides with Gallic charm over the formal cocktail bar, where you ponder your choice of dishes and await the summons of Tony Ferrario, the Restaurant Manager. The dining room has walls the soft red of the blush of a ripe peach, gleaming white table-cloths, and at night is lit by tall brass candlesticks with heavy glass shades. I found that a hot mousse of mushrooms in a port sauce was delicate and finely seasoned, a turban of assorted fish in a lobster butter sauce melted in the mouth, and ratatouille, separate courgettes, and potatoes faintly flavored with artichoke were all perfect. A slice of soft Italian meringue with slightly crunchy almost caramelized crystallized orange crumbled into it, flavored with Cointreau and served chilled, and a cup of excellent coffee, completed a superb meal. Chef Pierre Chevillard richly deserves his Michelin Guide star.

The owner, Martin Skan, has an outstanding team of managers and department heads, many of whom have been with him for anything up to eighteen years. It is their attention to every detail concerning the comfort of the guest that makes Chewton Glen such a very impressive place in which to stay.

Opposite: Chewton Glen's front door has welcomed many international guests eager to sample its famous cuisine (above). Overleaf: the colorful hallway and luxurious rooms are complemented by the magnificent grounds.

CHEWTON GLEN HOTEL, New Milton, Hampshire BH25 6QS. **Tel.** Highcliffe (04252) 5341. **Telex** 41456 CHGLEN G. **Owner** Martin Skan. **Open** All year. **Rooms** 33 double, 11 suites, all with bathroom (tub and shower each), color TV, direct-dial phone. **Facilities** Bar, bar/lounge with pianist, 2 other lounges, private board room, restaurant, boutique, snooker room, heated outdoor pool (summer only), all-weather tennis court, croquet, putting, 9-hole golf course, 30-acre grounds, incl. valley walk to sea and beach. Chauffeur service. **Restrictions** No dogs; no children under 7. **Terms** Expensive. **Credit cards** All major cards. **Getting there** M3/M27 Exit 1 (marked Lyndhurst). After Lyndhurst, follow signs to A35 (marked Christchurch and Bournemouth). Ignore all signs for New Milton. After about 11 miles, turn L for Walkford and Highcliffe opposite Cat and Fiddle pub. Go through Walkford, after which take 2nd L (Chewton Farm Rd), hotel on R. About 2 hrs. **Helicopter landing** Yes ("a few days notice"). **Of local interest** Golf, sailing, cruising, riding, fishing, and horse-drawn cart rides; Broadlands; Exbury Gardens; Beaulieu (house and Motor Museum). Historic Ships Museum, Portsmouth. **Whole day expeditions** Winchester; Salisbury; Hardy's Dorset. See hotel's own guide. **Refreshments** Red Lion, Boldre; Rose and Thistle, Rockbourne; Three Lions, Stuckton (Fordingbridge). **Dining out** La Provence, Gordleton Mill; Old Manor House, Romsey.

A famous architect's costly showpiece

Surrounded in spring by a sea of pink and white apple blossom, Little Thakeham looks like a typical early English stone manor house, with later additions in red brick hung with Sussex tiles. But appearances deceive: though Tudor in style, with a Great Hall, Minstrels' Gallery, huge fireplace, and upstairs Long Gallery for exercise on rainy days, Little Thakeham was designed by the notable architect Sir Edwin Lutyens at the turn of this century for a wealthy Brighton businessman. Lutyens used only the finest materials and most skilled craftsmen, with glorious results. Throughout the house are solid oak, shining quarry tiles, hand-crafted iron door hinges and latches, and polished stone floors. The garden, laid out by the famous Gertrude Jekyll, has rose walks – note the millstones set into the paths – shrubberies, grassy recreation areas for tennis and croquet, and a pergola leading the eye to the orchards and woods beyond. All this was to be for a family of five with thirteen servants, but unfortunately the lavish use of only the best bankrupted the businessman.

The present owners, Tim and Pauline Ratcliff, have supplemented the original bedrooms by converting day and night nurseries and attics into delightful individual bedchambers, with charming wallpapers, attractive fabrics, and modern bathrooms. They have almost finished restoring the garden (adding a swimming pool discreetly), but have not replaced the eighty-year-old climbing roses, chosen by the designer. They have hunted out furniture contemporary with the house, and even found the Lutyens-designed original sideboard, now back in its proper place in the dining room.

Tim Ratcliff feels very strongly about using only the best English ingredients cooked in the delicious traditional manner. Lobster, halibut, and sole come from the south coast, and the famous Southdown lamb is raised only a few miles away. There are Hampshire melons, wild game from Sussex, and thick yellow cream from a nearby Jersey herd. Local market gardens and the surrounding orchards provide fresh vegetables and fruit; herbs are from the gardens. The wine-list is a connoisseur's selection, and includes some exceptional vintages. Sitting with fellow guests in front of the big log fire after an excellent meal, I found them unanimous in their praise of the food and of the relaxing house-party atmosphere. The next morning, faced with pouring rain, people contentedly curled up with magazines in the comfortable armchairs, or happily wandered through the spacious house, examining with delight its features and contents. On fine days there is all the marvellous Hampshire and Sussex countryside to explore as well as Roman Chichester's medieval cathedral and modern boutiques, and Brighton's fantastic Royal Pavilion, gracious Regency terraces, and intricate Lanes, a lure for all antique hunters.

Opposite, above, and overleaf: Little Thakeham house and gardens are the creation of two geniuses – Edwin Lutyens and Gertrude Jekyll – and their heritage has been lovingly preserved.

LITTLE THAKEHAM, Merrywood Lane, Storrington, West Sussex RH20 3HE. **Tel.** Storrington (09066) 4416. **Telex** No. **Owners** Tim and Pauline Ratcliff. **Open** All year, except 10 days following 24 Dec. **Rooms** 10 double, all with bathroom (with handshower), color TV, direct-dial phone, radio. **Facilities** Bar, lounge, dining room, pool, grass tennis court, croquet lawn, 5-acre grounds. Courtesy cars by arrangement. **Restrictions** No dogs. **Terms** Medium. NB Bookings of 2 nights or longer preferred. **Credit cards** All major cards (personal checks preferred).

Getting there A24. After Ashington, watch for Thakeham turning on R. Bear R at fork. Hotel is about 1½ miles from turning. About 1½ hrs. **Helicopter landing** Yes (24 hrs notice). **Of local interest** Horse racing at Goodwood. Arundel Castle, Petworth House, Brighton, Lewes, Chichester. **Whole day expeditions** Winchester, Chartwell (Churchill's home), Leonards Lee gardens, Gilbert White's Selborne. **Refreshments** Many pleasant country pubs in the area – ask at hotel for suggestions. **Dining out** Manley's, Storrington.

Live like a lord

Newick Park, home of Viscount Brentford, is not a hotel as such, and you cannot drive up to the front door expecting to find a bed for that night. It is a member of the Heritage Circle, a small group of owners of some of England's loveliest historic houses who welcome visitors wishing to experience day-to-day life in what is essentially a family home. Arrangements must be made well in advance, by telephone or letter, with Lady Brentford.

Newick Park is a handsome 18th-century mansion whose famous garden includes shrubs brought from China at the end of the last century, and 300-year-old sweet chestnut trees. From the moment you arrive you are a family guest. There is no drinks book to sign, no menu, no extras except any telephone calls or whatever you might wish to leave for the staff. Your account will be left for you discreetly in the Visitors' Book which you sign on departure. My pleasant bedroom was called the Tulip Room, with tall windows looking over parkland, an extremely comfortable bed, central heating, a clock radio, tea and coffee-making facilities, and a space heater, electric blanket, and hot-water bottle for a sudden cold snap. It had pink walls, rose-motif chintz, its own bathroom across the corridor and the sort of collection of varied antiques found only in English country houses. Do not expect television or telephone in your room – they are available elsewhere.

Dinner is served formally in the elegantly proportioned dining room at a long polished table graced with flowers and family silver. Crispin Brentford sits at its head, listening with a lawyer's courteous attention to the conversation. Behind him hangs the life-size portrait of his grandfather Sir William Joynson-Hicks, First Viscount, sometime Home Secretary, and for long a political rival of Sir Winston Churchill. Another likeness is of a lady who scandalized the family by eloping through the pantry window with the gentleman whose picture hangs beside hers. Gill Brentford serves traditional English

dishes, delicious as only home cooking can be: smoked fish, tender lamb, beef, or duck from the estate, locally grown vegetables, and family-favorite desserts of trifle, pies, or tarts, with fresh fruit from their orchards and perfectly selected cheeses to follow.

The hosts tend to retire early, as Lord Brentford is a partner in the family law firm, and Lady Brentford assists in a commodity trading company, another family business. Having only recently inherited the estate, they are also very busy improving the grounds. They are charming, friendly, and attentive hosts, with an international outlook (their eldest daughter has been educated in the USA). A footnote: if necessary, arrangements can be made to accommodate chauffeurs in the village.

Opposite and above: attractive gardens and gracious interiors at Newick Park add to the pleasure of sampling the daily life of the aristocracy.

NEWICK PARK, Newick, East Sussex BN8 4SB. **Tel.** Newick (082 572) 2915. **Telex** 268014 JHICKS G. **Owners** Viscount and Viscountess Brentford. **Open** Most of the year. **Rooms** 11 twin, 14 double, 3 single, 17 with bathrooms (15 en suite, 2 private). No TV or phone in bedrooms. **Facilities** Hall, drawing room, library, dining room. Guest phone and TV. Pool, tennis court, croquet. **Restrictions** No children under 7. No dogs. **Terms** Medium. **Credit cards** Visa/Amex. **Getting there** M23, A23, E on A272 to Newick. About 1½ hrs. **Helicopter landing** Yes (2 days notice). **Of local interest** Glyndebourne opera (May to August); Knole; Lewes; Brighton. **Whole day expeditions** Canterbury; Bodiam Castle; Leeds Castle; Sissinghurst and Scotney gardens. **Refreshments** Rose and Crown, Fletching; Peacock, Piltdown. **Dining out** Horsted Place, Uckfield (see p.95).

An ancient family home close to Glyndebourne

Peter Dunn has travelled all over the world, firstly as a serving officer in World War II, later as a consultant engineer. His wife, Jane, and their lively and enterprising children have often gone with him, or set off independently to China or India. Familiar with the needs of travellers, they are also accomplished hosts. When I stayed at Stone House, Jane, with characteristic lack of fuss, and in the middle of a busy season, had just thrown an "Indian raj" party for three hundred guests to celebrate her silver wedding; a marquee had been erected on the lawn and the house was filled with exotic flowers.

Stone House was built in the early 1300s for Peter's family. Never having been sold, it has no deeds, which confuses officialdom when Peter needs to show title to their 1200 acres. The heart of the house is the ancient low-beamed dining room, hung with family portraits, filled with fine china and gleaming silver. It has an inglenook and a bread oven; the fine panelling, huge sideboard, and long polished table are of time-darkened oak. The massive solid oak staircase in the back hall was built in 1535; the front hall, with a black and white marble checkerboard floor and gracefully curving stairs, was added in 1778, together with the stately high-ceilinged drawing room and welcoming book-lined library. The bedrooms at the front are lofty, with four-poster beds, draped and smocked, one in soft pinks and blues, the other in warm yellows and browns. One marble bathroom has space enough for sofa and chairs, the other, down some steps, is wood-panelled. The bedrooms at the back of the house are smaller, though equally charming, with creaky sloping floors, low ceilings, and beams. All have linen with drawn-thread work, baskets of top-quality fresh fruit, freshly-baked shortbread beside the bed, and lovely views over parkland and lake.

This is a private house, offering accommodation for guests in three bedrooms, together with snacks and excellent full breakfasts, but no dinner. Occasionally, however, the Dunns let the whole house to a shooting party, small conference, or a group of friends, in which case seven bedrooms are available, a boardroom can be set up, and Jane and her children provide whatever meals are required. Both individual guests and groups can enjoy the Dunns' speciality, magnificent picnic hampers filled with crystal, fine china and gourmet dishes, for opera-lovers visiting Glyndebourne. Peter and Jane are kind and thoughtful hosts and good organizers, their children are helpful and friendly, and the staff are charming, so that you feel from the first moment that you are staying with old friends. This fascinating house, set in glorious countryside, is a joy to visit.

Lustrous wood, antique silver and magnificent portraits fill the dining room (above). Stone House is a delightful mix of architectural styles (opposite, above) with a relaxed and elegant atmosphere (opposite, below).

STONE HOUSE, Rushlake Green, Heathfield, East Sussex TN21 9QJ. **Tel.** Rushlake Green (0435) 830233. **Telex** 957210 RLT G. **Owners** Peter and Jane Dunn. **Open** All year, but closed for all but shooting parties, small conferences, etc. from Nov.–end March. **Rooms** 3 double, all with bathroom (2 including hand shower), color TV, radio, direct-dial phone. NB 4 further rooms, similarly equipped, are available if whole house booked. **Facilities** Drawing room, library, panelled dining room, billiard room, grounds and gardens with lake, 1200-acre estate adjacent. Small conference facilities. Croquet lawn. Glyndebourne (May–Aug.). Picnics, fishing, shooting, private visits to stately homes (all by arrangement). **Restrictions** No dogs in public rooms, no children under 9, no smoking in dining room. No dinner or lunch except snacks, unless by prior arrangement. **Terms** Medium to expensive. **Credit cards** None. **Getting there** M25/A21 S to Hurst Green. R to Burwash, L to Woods Corner. R on B2096 towards Heathfield, take L fork marked Rushlake Green. Entrance from village green. About 2 hrs. **Helicopter landing** Yes. **Of local interest** Burwash; Battle; Hurstmonceaux. Netherfield Place, Battle; Horsted Place, Uckfield (see p.95). **Whole day expeditions** Chartwell (Churchill's home); Knole; gardens at Scotney, Leonards Lee and Nymans; Canterbury; Sandwich (famous golf course). **Refreshments** Horse and Groom, Rushlake Green; William the Conqueror, Rye harbor; Star Inn, Heathfield. **Dining out** Blacksmith's Restaurant, Battle; Gravetye Manor, Nr East Grinstead.

An ornate Victorian masterpiece

Horsted Place is an imposing mansion built in 1850 for a wealthy London merchant. A masterpiece of ornate Victorian Gothic, it has towers, tall brick chimneys and a great central Gallery running through its entire length, from which rises an imposing carved oak staircase designed by Augustus Pugin, whose work richly ornaments the Houses of Parliament. The public rooms are high-ceilinged and full of light from the large windows. There is a book-lined library with a secret door into an enclosed courtyard with a fountain, a gracious dining room, and glorious gardens designed by Sir Geoffrey Jellicoe. The heated covered pool has glass doors all along one side which open to flowerbeds and terraces. The spacious suites are comfortably furnished with settees and chairs, the beds have soft down pillows and crisp linen sheets, the large closets have linen bags for laundry, and the bathrooms are splendid. If you choose to take breakfast in your room, it will be set out on a table with a linen cloth, silver and flowers. Such attentive service is appropriate in what was until recently the private home of Prince Philip's Treasurer. It was often visited by the Queen and other members of the royal family, who would stroll through the grounds along a path specially made for privacy, to the pew reserved for them in the little Norman village church nearby.

I arrived to find the house full of flowers, and fires burning brightly in all the elaborately carved fireplaces. The very helpful staff call guests by name, strengthening the feeling of being a member of an agreeable house party rather than a guest at a hotel. Manager Guy Rigby, previously with the London Ritz, writes a personal letter of welcome to each arriving guest, enclosing a note of the hotel's

amenities, and urging one not to hesitate to ask for anything further one might want. The tea that I requested arrived swiftly. Drinks are offered in the drawing room before dinner, while guests study the short but varied menu and the wine list, which offers an enormous selection of sensibly priced wines. I enjoyed a quail salad, a mousseline of scallop and turbot, Scottish venison with a red wine sauce, and a trio of home-made sorbets.

The hotel's setting is totally peaceful: at night the only sound was an owl hooting in the nearby woods. All about lies the beautiful Sussex countryside, and there are views to the gently rolling South Downs. The famous Glyndebourne opera house is only five miles away, and the whole area is known for being good riding, shooting, and fishing country. Leaving, I planned my return: perhaps one year I will spend Christmas here and walk the Queen's path to Midnight Service in the tiny church.

The decorative brickwork and spectacular Gothic exterior of Horsted Place contain charming, light-filled rooms (above, the dining room).

HORSTED PLACE, Little Horsted, Uckfield, East Sussex, TN22 5TS. **Tel.** Uckfield (0825) 75581. **Telex** 95548 HORSTD G. **Owners** Horsted Hotels Ltd. **Manager** Guy Rigby. **Open** All year except two weeks in Jan. **Rooms** 14 suites, 3 small doubles, all with bathroom (including wall-mounted shower), 2 direct-dial phones (1 in bedroom area, 1 in sitting area), 1 or 2 color TVs, similarly arranged, radio. **Facilities** Drawing room, morning room, library, dining room, small conference facilities, elevator, 8-acre formal gardens in 23-acre parkland, croquet lawn, all-weather tennis court, heated indoor pool. Fishing, riding, clay pigeon shooting, golf by arrangement. **Restrictions** No pets, no children under 7, no pipes or cigars in dining room.

Terms Expensive. Includes full breakfast. Winter sporting breaks Oct.–March. **Credit cards** All major cards. **Getting there** M25/M23, Exit 10, A264 to East Grinstead, A22 to Uckfield, round ring road, R at 3rd traffic circle, A26. Hotel 100 yards on R. **Helicopter landing** Yes. **Of local interest** Glyndebourne opera house (May to August); Sissinghurst gardens; Hever Castle; Sheffield Park Gardens. **Whole day expeditions** Many Sussex and Kent gardens nearby; good information from hotel. **Refreshments** Many picturesque pubs; enquire from hotel. **Dining out** Gravetye Manor, Nr East Grinstead; The Sundial, Hurstmonceaux.

Index